JORDAN
TRAVEL GUIDE

The Ultimate Travel Book To Uncovering Jordan's Hidden Gem

Patrick Wilson

Table of Contents

Brief History

Jordan, an exotic country in the center of the Middle East, possesses a rich and captivating history that reaches back to ancient times. As a tourist seeing Jordan's historical landmarks, you'll be engaged in a fascinating voyage through the years, watching the rise and fall of many civilizations that have left their mark on this region.

The earliest known history of Jordan may be traced back to the Paleolithic epoch, with evidence of human habitation extending back over 250,000 years. Throughout the years, the region was home to various prominent ancient civilizations, including the Ammonites, Moabites, and Edomites.

One of the most famous times in Jordan's history was during the reign of the Nabataeans, who constructed their capital at the splendid city of Petra in about the 4th century BC. Petra, a UNESCO World Heritage Site, was a significant hub for trade, culture, and religion, benefiting from the caravan routes that connected it to distant places. The Nabataeans were talented architects who sculpted spectacular facades into the pink sandstone cliffs, creating stunning structures that still astonish visitors today.

In the 1st century AD, the Roman Empire extended its dominance over the region, and the city of Jerash flourished as a provincial Roman metropolis. Known as Gerasa in ancient times, Jerash features extremely well-preserved Greco-Roman architecture, including a huge hippodrome, temples, and theaters, making it one of the most spectacular Roman monuments in the Middle East.

With the advent of Christianity, Jordan became a vital element of the Holy Land, and significant biblical events occurred within its borders. The River Jordan, where John the Baptist baptized Jesus, remains a key pilgrimage place for Christians worldwide.

In the 7th century AD, Islamic Arab troops captured Jordan, and it became part of the Islamic Caliphate. The Umayyad dynasty chose the city of Amman as their administrative seat, and the Amman Citadel still exists as a witness to this era, showing a blend of Roman, Byzantine, and Islamic architecture.

Throughout the next centuries, Jordan witnessed the rise and fall of several dynasties, notably the Crusaders and the Mamluks. The Ottoman Empire later acquired control of the region in the 16th century, leaving its architectural heritage in sites like the Ajloun Castle and the Ottoman-era buildings in Madaba.

In the early 20th century, Jordan came under British influence, becoming part of the British Mandate of Palestine. After the end of World War II, Jordan gained independence in 1946, forming the Hashemite Kingdom of Jordan with King Abdullah I as its first king.

Jordan has been a key player in regional affairs, playing a role in the Arab-Israeli conflict and housing waves of refugees from neighboring nations. Despite the problems, Jordan has maintained a generally stable and calm atmosphere, becoming a popular destination for tourists seeking a blend of history, culture, and natural beauty.

As a visitor visiting Jordan, you'll have the opportunity to discover ancient sites, experience traditional Bedouin culture, float in the healing waters of the Dead Sea, and wonder at the rocky landscapes of Wadi Rum. Jordan's history is carved into every corner of the country, delivering a profound and immersive experience that ties the past with the present, making it a journey of discovery and wonder that you'll love for a lifetime.

Geography

Covering an area of approximately 89,342 square kilometers, Jordan is surrounded by Israel and the West Bank to the west, Syria to the north, Iraq to the northeast, and Saudi Arabia to the south and southeast. The country's landscape is distinguished by a unique blend of deserts, mountains, and valleys, each contributing to its own environmental and climatic conditions.

One of the major elements of Jordan's topography is the Great Rift Valley, which spans through the country from the north to the south. This geological feature is a product of the tectonic action that generated the rift millions of years ago. The Jordan Valley, a portion of the Great Rift Valley, is a fertile region with the Jordan River flowing through it. This river is not only historically significant but also acts as a vital water resource for the country.

To the west of the Jordan Valley lies the western highlands, known as the Hill Country. This region is characterized by undulating hills and plateaus, delivering a warmer environment compared to the harsh desert areas. It is also the location of Jordan's capital city, Amman, and other major metropolitan hubs.

The eastern section of Jordan is dominated by the Arabian Desert, a large expanse of sand and stony terrain. The desert climate is harsh, with hot summers and chilly winters. However, despite its dry environment, this region has been inhabited for thousands of years, and ancient archaeological monuments, such as Petra and Jerash, bore evidence of the historical significance of the area.

The southern area of Jordan is home to Wadi Rum, a UNESCO World Heritage Site, noted for its beautiful sandstone mountains and dramatic desert vistas. This area has drawn travelers and explorers for ages, and today it remains a popular destination for travelers seeking outdoor adventures and cultural encounters.

Water scarcity is a serious concern in Jordan due to its limited water supplies and increasing population needs. The country mainly relies on groundwater and the Jordan River for its water supply, which leads to great strain on the ecosystem and the need for sustainable water management measures.

Jordan's geographical location has greatly influenced its historical and cultural development. Being situated at the crossroads of old trade routes, the area has been a melting pot of numerous civilizations, including Nabateans, Romans, Byzantines, and Arabs. This rich past is evident in the various archaeological sites and ancient ruins strewn around the country.

Conclusion

Jordan's topography includes a tapestry of various landscapes, from the fertile Jordan Valley to the arid Arabian Desert and the spectacular mountains of Wadi Rum. The country's location at the crossroads of ancient civilizations has shaped its history and cultural heritage. However, the concerns of water shortage and environmental sustainability must be tackled to ensure a bright future for this unique and historically significant nation.

Tourists Must Know Things Before Visiting

Before visiting Jordan, travelers must be ready with important knowledge to make the most of their stay in this beautiful country. From its rich history to cultural standards, natural beauties, and practical suggestions, here's a thorough description of everything travelers need to know:

Culture
Culture plays a vital role in Jordanian society. Dress modestly, especially at religious sites and conservative areas. Greetings are vital, and it's normal to share pleasantries before getting down to business. Jordanians are recognized for their wonderful hospitality, and it is typical to be invited for tea or meals by locals.

Safety and Security
Jordan is generally regarded as secure for travelers, with a stable political situation. However, it's crucial to keep an eye on travel advisories and updates from your government. Exercise usual care, be aware of your surroundings, and observe local laws and customs.

Currency and Costs
The national currency is the Jordanian Dinar (JOD). Cash is widely accepted, however, credit cards are frequently utilized in big cities. It's important to take cash while visiting distant locations. Budget tourists can find reasonable lodging and cuisine, while luxury alternatives are available for those seeking a more opulent experience.

Religion and Customs

Islam is the primary religion in Jordan, and strict Islamic beliefs are revered throughout the country. Dress modestly, remove shoes before entering homes or mosques, and avoid public shows of affection. During the holy month of Ramadan, be conscious of fasting hours and be considerate of those keeping the fast.

Safety in the Desert

Exploring Jordan's desert areas may be an amazing experience, but it's crucial to emphasize safety. If you plan to embark on desert expeditions, always hire recognized guides or join organized groups. The desert's immensity and severe heat might be tough, so bring lots of drink, sun protection, and proper clothing.

Photography and Respect for Local Customs

Jordan is a photographer's dream, with its ancient ruins, arid landscapes, and attractive cities. However, it's crucial to be respectful when shooting images, especially of natives. Always request permission before photographing people, and avoid capturing sensitive sites, military installations, or anything that might be considered inappropriate.

Health Precautions

Before coming to Jordan, ensure you are up-to-date with standard immunizations. Depending on your itinerary and activities, additional vaccines or health measures might be necessary. It's essential to see a travel health clinic or your healthcare practitioner before your trip.

Respect for Environment and Heritage Sites

As a responsible tourist, respect for the environment and heritage places is vital. Avoid trash, and be mindful of your influence on sensitive ecosystems. When visiting historical sites, refrain from touching or climbing on ancient structures to maintain their integrity for future generations.

By immersing yourself in Jordan's rich history, seeing its natural beauties, and embracing its cultural heritage, you'll definitely make cherished memories and form lasting bonds with this magnificent country and its hospitable people. Remember, a well-informed visitor is a respectful and responsible one, capable of genuinely appreciating all that Jordan has to offer. Enjoy your adventure!

Best Touring Apps and websites

To make the most of your vacation, it's necessary to have access to the top touring applications and websites. Here are some of the finest applications and websites that enhance your trip experience in Jordan.

Visit Jordan's Official (*https://www.visitjordan.gov.jo/*): This official website from the Jordan Tourism Board is a wonderful starting point. It gives important information about tourist destinations, cultural activities, and practical travel suggestions. You may find details about popular places like Petra, Wadi Rum, and the Dead Sea, along with suggested itineraries and hotel alternatives.

Google Maps (*https://www.google.com/maps*): One of the most trustworthy navigation tools, Google Maps, works well in Jordan. It provides accurate directions, traffic updates, and nearby sites of interest. It's a crucial tool for touring towns like Amman and navigating the country's different terrain.

TripAdvisor (*https://www.tripadvisor.com/*): TripAdvisor is a widely-used tool for tourists to read reviews, find hotels, restaurants, and attractions. The website features a specific Jordan section that offers vital insights from fellow visitors and locals, letting you plan your schedule with confidence.

Jordan Pass (*https://www.jordanpass.jo/*): The Jordan Pass is an all-in-one ticket that provides you admission to several attractions across the country, including Petra, Jerash, and Wadi Rum. Purchasing the Jordan Pass online will save you both time and money during your vacation.

Airbnb (*https://www.airbnb.com/*): For a more authentic experience, consider using Airbnb to find unique accommodations, such as staying with local hosts in traditional Jordanian homes. It's a terrific way to immerse yourself in the local culture and create memorable memories.

Weather.com (*https://weather.com/*): Weather can play a crucial effect in your trip plans. Use Weather.com or other trusted weather apps to check the prediction and pack accordingly for your journey.

Uber and Careem: In big cities like Amman, Uber, and Careem are prominent ride-sharing services that offer convenient and reliable transportation options.

Instagram (*https://www.instagram.com/*): While not a specific travel app, Instagram is a valuable resource for discovering gorgeous spots in Jordan. Many tourists and influencers post amazing images and travel ideas that can inspire your own vacation.

Madain Project (*https://madainproject.com/*): This website is a useful resource for history aficionados. It gives thorough information about historical sites in Jordan, including archaeological discoveries and lesser-known ruins, allowing you to delve deeper into the country's rich legacy.

Jordan Trail (*https://jordantrail.org/*): If you're an avid hiker and nature lover, the Jordan Trail is a must-visit webpage. It includes thorough information about the 650-kilometer-long hiking trail that extends across the country, showing varied landscapes and connecting cultural landmarks.

Eat Like a Local (*https://www.eatlikealocal.com/*): This app allows you to explore Jordan's culinary scene with authenticity. It gives recommendations for local cafes, street food booths, and family-run restaurants, offering you a chance to enjoy traditional meals loved by locals.

Waze (*https://www.waze.com/*): For driving in Jordan, Waze is an outstanding navigation program that provides real-time information on traffic conditions, road closures, and alternate routes, helping you navigate effectively.

Meal Delivery Apps: When you want to taste local cuisine from the comfort of your lodging, consider using popular meal delivery apps like Talabat (https://www.talabat.com/jordan) or Carriage (https://www.trycarriage.com/).

XE Converter (*https://www.xe.com/currencyconverter/*): This program will come in handy when you need to convert your currencies to Jordanian Dinar (JOD) for effortless transactions.

Culture Trip (*https://theculturetrip.com/*): Culture Trip delivers comprehensive articles and guides about Jordan's cultural heritage, art, and traditions, helping you develop a greater understanding of the country.

Booking.com (*https://www.booking.com/*): Alongside other lodging options, Booking.com is a popular platform for locating hotels, resorts, and guesthouses across Jordan, offering a wide range of choices to meet your preferences and budget.

Remember, while these apps and websites are fantastic resources for your trip to Jordan, it's always wise to create a balance between technology and engaging with the local culture and people. Don't hesitate to interact with locals, try their advice, and immerse yourself fully in the unique experiences that Jordan has to offer.

Top Activities

Jordan offers a varied choice of physical outdoor activities for tourists, making it a dream destination for adventure fans. From the beautiful vistas of Wadi Rum to the ancient wonders of Petra, the country has a multitude of options to engage in adventurous and memorable adventures.

Wadi Rum Activities

Nestled in the heart of southern Jordan, Wadi Rum stands as a beautiful tribute to the raw splendor of nature. Often referred to as the "Valley of the Moon," this amazing desert scenery has grabbed the hearts of adventurers and outdoor enthusiasts from around the globe. With its beautiful sandstone formations, wide canyons, and rich history, Wadi Rum provides a plethora of physical outdoor activities that cater to every style of traveler seeking an adrenaline rush and a spiritual connection with nature.

Rock Climbing

For those who desire the excitement of mounting huge rock formations, Wadi Rum presents a rock climber's paradise. The steep sandstone walls, some reaching heights of over 1,000 feet, challenge climbers of all levels. The brilliant red and orange tones of the rocks contrast against the turquoise sky, providing a visual spectacle as climbers ascend the natural crags. Jebel Rum and Jebel Um Ishrin are two of the most prominent summits, with routes that range from beginner-friendly to expert-level difficulties. Accompanied by expert local guides, climbers can safely explore these vertical beauties, forging not only a physical achievement but also a deep sense of success.

Hiking

For those who prefer to keep their feet on the ground, Wadi Rum features an extensive network of trekking routes that crisscross over its immense expanse. From peaceful walks to difficult treks, there is a trail for every adventurer. The trails often lead to secret oases, old petroglyphs, and small valleys that reflect the intricate geological history of the region. The Khazali Canyon, with its narrow walls studded with inscriptions from past civilizations, is a particularly popular trekking site. Whether it's a short stroll to watch a sunrise over the desert or a multi-day excursion deep into the heart of Wadi Rum, hikers are rewarded with spectacular views and a profound connection to the land's past.

Jeep Tours

For those seeking a more comfortable yet equally exhilarating experience, Jeep trips provide a unique way to explore the expanse of Wadi Rum. Local Bedouin guides, thoroughly aware of the area, navigate through the complicated maze of sand dunes and rock formations. The jeeps gently glide over the sand, carrying passengers to distant and otherwise inaccessible sections of the desert. A popular route is the Seven Pillars of Wisdom, made famous by T.E. Lawrence's books. As the sun sets over the horizon, throwing a warm glow over the landscape, travelers are left awe-inspired by the pure beauty and peacefulness of Wadi Rum.

Hot Air Ballooning

For those who prefer to take their journey to the skies, hot air ballooning provides a unique perspective of Wadi Rum's breathtaking magnificence. Drifting softly over the desert bottom, passengers are rewarded with panoramic vistas of the enormous sand dunes, towering rock formations, and ancient valleys below. The feeling of serenity and awe is unrivaled as the early morning light covers the countryside with a delicate, golden color. Hot air ballooning offers a calm counterpoint to the more physically taxing activities, allowing guests to appreciate the beauty of Wadi Rum in a tranquil setting.

Camping

To complete the immersive experience, camping in Wadi Rum is necessary. Bedouin-style camps dot the desert, providing guests a chance to sleep under the starlit sky in traditional goat-hair tents. The serene silence of the desert night, broken only by the crackling of a campfire, is an extraordinary experience. As the Milky Way extends across the heavens, travelers are reminded of their place in the immense cosmos. Many camps also serve traditional Bedouin dinners, allowing guests to taste the flavors of the region while being immersed in the warmth of Bedouin hospitality.

Canyoning in Wadi Mujib

Nestled in the heart of Jordan, Wadi Mujib stands as a tribute to the majesty of nature's raw strength. This stunning gorge, known as the "Grand Canyon of Jordan," offers a wealth of intense physical outdoor activities that draw adventure enthusiasts from around the world. From canyoning to hiking, and from rappelling to swimming, Wadi Mujib is a paradise for people who want an adrenaline rush amidst stunning landscapes.

Stretching along the eastern borders of the Dead Sea, Wadi Mujib is a natural wonder that has been carved over millions of years by the force of water. With towering sandstone cliffs, turquoise pools, and flowing waterfalls, the canyon is a wonderful spectacle of nature's handiwork. But beneath its scenic attractiveness is a playground for outdoor lovers willing to immerse themselves in a realm of physical challenges.

Canyoning is the definitive activity in Wadi Mujib, allowing guests to experience the depths of the canyon in a unique and intimate way. Equipped with helmets, life jackets, and the instruction of professional instructors, adventurers trek through small corridors, slide down polished rock chutes, and wade through waist-deep water. The joy of defeating each challenge is matched only by the thrill of discovering hidden rooms and experiencing the ever-changing hues of the canyon walls.

Hiking in Wadi Mujib gives an opportunity to connect with nature on a different level. The pathways weave across the canyon's various habitats, from harsh desert terrain to lush oases. The Siq trail is a popular choice, carrying hikers through the middle of the gorge. As they walk through the riverbed, hikers are rewarded with vistas of the spectacular fauna that calls this harsh terrain home, including ibexes and other bird species.

Rappelling down the towering cliffs of Wadi Mujib is an experience that blends heart-pounding adrenaline with the satisfaction of mastering a physical obstacle. The adrenaline rush is equaled only by the spectacular panoramic views that unveil as participants gradually lower themselves down the steep sides of the canyon walls. This exercise involves both mental fortitude and a feeling of adventure, making it a memorable highlight for many tourists.

One of the most interesting elements of Wadi Mujib is its aquatic environment. The river that flows through the gorge creates natural pools and waterfalls that are great for swimming and cooling off after a day of exercise. The cool, crystal-clear waters provide a refreshing break from the

Jordanian heat, and the sensation of swimming in a canyon surrounded by towering rocks is truly incomparable.

For those seeking a multi-day excursion, Wadi Mujib also offers camping alternatives. Sleeping under the star-studded desert sky, surrounded by ancient geological wonders, is an experience that forges a deep connection with the natural world. As dawn comes, the rising light sheds its golden glow on the sandstone cliffs, producing a bizarre and awe-inspiring picture.

Safety is of fundamental concern in any outdoor activity, and Wadi Mujib is no different. Local guides and qualified employees are on hand to ensure that tourists are outfitted with the required gear, well-informed about the challenges that lie ahead, and able to navigate the terrain safely. It's vital for visitors to comply with guidelines, follow instructions, and protect the fragile environment to preserve the beauty of Wadi Mujib for centuries to come.

Snorkeling and Diving

Snorkeling and diving in Jordan offer beautiful underwater experiences that allow travelers to discover the Red Sea's magnificent marine life and underwater sceneries. From vivid coral reefs to historic shipwrecks, this Middle Eastern destination has an aquatic wonderland waiting to be found.

Snorkeling
Snorkeling is a popular aquatic activity in Jordan, particularly in areas like Aqaba, where the Red Sea's crystal-clear waters provide an excellent setting for beginners and experienced snorkelers alike. The ease and accessibility of snorkeling make it an attractive option for tourists who wish to witness the underwater beauty without the complications of diving equipment and qualifications.

Equipped with a mask, snorkel, and fins, devotees can float on the water's surface while staring into the colorful world underneath. The Red Sea is famed for its magnificent coral reefs, filled with an assortment of marine life, including colorful fish, graceful rays, and even the occasional turtle. Snorkelers can bask in the spectacular sight of these aquatic critters rushing through the coral gardens, surrounded by a spectrum of hues that dazzle the sea.

Snorkeling in Jordan also offers a unique opportunity to experience the synergy between desert and sea. The shoreline is flanked by stunning mountain scenery, creating a striking backdrop to the underwater adventure. Whether it's the protected coves or the more adventurous open-water sites, the Red Sea's snorkeling spots accommodate a range of interests and ability levels.

Diving
For those seeking a deeper immersion into the underwater environment, diving in Jordan gives a portal to extraordinary marine encounters. With the Gulf of Aqaba offering a broad choice of dive locations, including beautiful coral reefs and ancient wrecks, divers are in for a memorable experience.

Aqaba's underwater scenery is distinguished by vivid coral formations, which are not only magnificent to behold but also provide essential habitats for many marine creatures. Divers may explore the various nooks and crevices of these reefs, seeing fascinating marine animals like nudibranchs and seahorses hiding within.

One of the most captivating aspects of diving in Jordan is the presence of ancient wrecks. The Tank Dive Site, for instance, is home to a sunken military tank that now acts as an artificial reef, offering a unique underwater attraction. These submerged treasures offer a look into the region's history while offering a playground for aquatic life to flourish.

Dive locations such as the Cedar Pride Wreck provide not only an opportunity for underwater fun but also a chance to contribute to marine conservation efforts. The Eco Dive Center in Aqaba, for instance, focuses on sustainable diving practices that prioritize the protection of vulnerable marine habitats.

It's worth mentioning that while snorkeling is quite accessible to most people, diving requires adequate training and certification. Diving centers in Jordan offer a range of training for beginners to advanced divers, ensuring safety and competency in underwater exploration.

Swimming in the Dead Sea

For travelers seeking an unusual aquatic encounter, few sites can beat the otherworldly feeling of swimming in the Dead Sea. Nestled between Israel and Jordan, this unique body of water is famed for its extreme salinity and extraordinary buoyancy.

The Dead Sea, known in Hebrew as the "Yam Ha-Melakh" and in Arabic as the "Bahr Lut," is not exactly a sea but a hypersaline lake. It is noted for its incredibly high salt concentration, which reaches around 30-35%, more than ten times that of typical saltwater. This salinity is owing to the fact that the lake has no outlet; water rushes in from the Jordan River and other sources but has no means to depart except through evaporation, leaving the minerals and salts behind.

The most striking part of swimming in the Dead Sea is the extraordinary buoyancy it affords. This phenomenon happens due to the high salt concentration, which effectively increases the water's density. As a result, anyone entering the water will find themselves effortlessly floating on the surface, even if they have no prior swimming expertise. Tourists sometimes enjoy in the bizarre sense of being suspended in the water, effortlessly reclining with a book or newspaper in hand, an experience that defies the laws of physics and creates an indelible memory.

But while the Dead Sea promises a spectacular trip, it also comes with certain considerations. The water's salt can cause discomfort if it comes into contact with the eyes or any open cuts, leading to a stinging feeling. It's essential to avoid immersing the head totally and to use caution while entering the water. Similarly, while the minerals in the water are recognized for their possible medicinal benefits, extended contact to the hypersaline environment may not be good for everyone, particularly those with specific medical issues. Consulting a healthcare professional before taking a dive is a sensible approach.

The area around the Dead Sea has a rich historical and cultural value. It's a location of contrasts, where the modern and ancient cohabit. Tourists can experience the luxury of spa resorts that have cropped up along the beach, offering mud treatments and salt scrubs that utilize the lake's mineral-rich mud. These treatments are not only calming but are also known to provide different skin advantages.

For history aficionados, the Dead Sea region is home to historic monuments such as Masada, a stronghold erected by King Herod atop a hill, and Qumran, where the Dead Sea Scrolls were found in the mid-20th century. Exploring these locations adds a layer of depth to the journey, providing insights into the region's historical and cultural significance.

In recent years, there has been increased concern about the environmental difficulties facing the Dead Sea. The water levels have been lowering due to reasons like diminished water intake from the Jordan River, industrial activities, and climate change. Efforts have been made to address this issue, with governments in the region considering various techniques to maintain the water levels and preserve this natural beauty for future generations of tourists to enjoy.

Conclusion
Jordan is a refuge for outdoor enthusiasts, offering a varied assortment of physical activities that cater to different interests and skill levels. Whether it's discovering ancient wonders, climbing through gorges, diving into the Red Sea, or relaxing in the Dead Sea, the country's natural beauty and historical treasures combine for an amazing adventure. With its warm warmth and rich past, Jordan is certainly a gem for travellers seeking an amazing and physically active vacation.

Dialects and Language

As a major tourist destination in the Middle East, understanding the numerous dialects and languages spoken in Jordan can substantially enhance one's travel experience.

Arabic serves as the official language of Jordan and is extensively spoken throughout the country. However, it's crucial to remember that the spoken Arabic in Jordan may differ greatly from the Modern Standard Arabic (MSA) taught in schools and used in formal settings. The colloquial variety of Arabic, known as Jordanian Arabic, is the most popular dialect and the one visitors are likely to meet in regular conversations.

Jordanian Arabic is recognized for its unusual vocabulary, pronunciation, and idiomatic idioms, which could be tough for non-native speakers to grasp first. However, locals often appreciate tourists making an effort to speak in their original language, even if it's just a few simple phrases.

In addition to Arabic, English is widely understood and spoken in Jordan, especially in metropolitan areas, as it is taught in schools and used in commerce and tourism. This makes traveling and getting around much easier for English-speaking tourists, as they can rely on English to negotiate numerous circumstances.

Apart from Arabic and English, there are other minority languages spoken in Jordan, representing the varied cultural backgrounds of its inhabitants. One such language is Circassian, spoken predominantly by the Circassian community, descendants of people who migrated from the

Caucasus in the 19th century. Though less frequent than Arabic or English, hearing Circassian spoken in certain places of Jordan is not uncommon.

Another minority language is Armenian, spoken by the Armenian community in the country. The Armenian language has been preserved through centuries, and some of the older generation might still use it in their everyday contacts.

Additionally, a small percentage of Jordanians, notably in urban locations, may speak some Western languages like French or German, owing to their education or international exposure. However, these cases are rather rare, and English remains the most useful language for travelers to connect with locals.

Jordan's linguistic diversity is a tribute to its historical and geographical significance. Throughout history, the region has been a crossroads for numerous civilizations and cultures, contributing to the variety of languages present today. While Arabic serves as the major language of identity and culture, the preservation of minority languages illustrates the country's commitment to pluralism and inclusion.

For travelers interested in language acquisition or cultural immersion, there are language schools and cultural institutes in large towns like Amman that provide Arabic classes for foreigners. Learning some basic Arabic phrases can tremendously enrich the trip experience and establish links with the local population.

Conclusion
Jordan features a unique blend of languages and dialects that mirror its rich background. While Arabic serves as the official

language and Jordanian Arabic dominates daily interactions, English is commonly known and used, making it convenient for English-speaking tourists. The presence of minority languages like Circassian and Armenian gives more richness to Jordan's linguistic landscape, showing the country's commitment to maintaining its rich cultural legacy. Embracing and comprehending these linguistic differences can enrich a tourist's experience, establishing deeper connections with the warm and inviting people of Jordan.

Weather

Jordan receives a broad range of climatic conditions due to its geographical location, which contains a mix of arid deserts, high plateaus, and the Dead Sea depression. The country's climate is characterized by scorching summers, mild winters, and large differences in temperature and precipitation throughout different locations. Understanding the weather in Jordan is vital for travelers planning their vacation to ensure a pleasant and happy trip.

Summer (June through September)
During summer, Jordan is noted for its searing heat, with temperatures climbing above 40°C (104°F) in several parts of the country. The desert locations, like Wadi Rum and Petra, can be particularly tough for tourists due to the intense aridity. Coastal areas like Aqaba also endure high temperatures, making it appropriate for beach activities.

Autumn (October through November)
Autumn is a wonderful time to visit Jordan since the weather becomes more temperate and pleasant. The blazing heat of July gradually declines, and temperatures vary between 20°C to 30°C (68°F to 86°F). This season allows travelers to experience the archaeological sites and natural settings peacefully.

Winter (December through February)
Winter in Jordan is comparatively mild compared to other regions having a Mediterranean climate. However, temperatures can dip to roughly 5°C to 10°C (41°F to 50°F), especially during the night. Snowfall is not unusual in higher

heights like Amman, Ajloun, and Madaba, providing a stunning environment that draws winter enthusiasts.

Spring (March through May)
Spring is another good time to visit Jordan since the weather gets increasingly nice. The temperatures climb gradually, ranging between 15°C to 25°C (59°F to 77°F), while the surroundings transform into bright colors due to blooming flowers and foliage. This season is great for exploring nature reserves, hiking routes, and enjoying outdoor activities.

Rainfall
Rainfall in Jordan is modest, with the majority falling between November and March. The coastal areas receive limited rainfall, whereas the hilly regions and northern portions experience significantly higher precipitation. Tourists should be prepared for occasional rain during the winter months.

The Dead Sea
The Dead Sea region has its unique microclimate, marked by high temperatures year-round and exceptionally low humidity. Summer temperatures can surpass 45°C (113°F) near the Dead Sea, making it necessary for tourists to stay hydrated and avoid vigorous activity during peak hours.

Aqaba
Aqaba, located in the southernmost section of Jordan along the Red Sea, offers a peculiar climate. It enjoys pleasant temperatures throughout the year, making it a favorite location for beachgoers and water sports aficionados.

Conclusion
Understanding the weather trends in Jordan is vital for travelers planning their vacation. Summer offers blistering

heat, while fall and spring offer more moderate temperatures and gorgeous vistas. Winter is typically moderate, however, some locations may see snowfall. Tourists should consider the distinct microclimates of specific places, such as the Dead Sea and Aqaba. Regardless of the season, packing suitable clothing, staying hydrated, and arranging outdoor activities wisely can ensure a pleasurable and safe experience while experiencing the intriguing country of Jordan.

Getting Here

When organizing a vacation to Jordan, one needs to know about the numerous transportation choices to visit this wonderful nation. Here's how to get to Jordan as a tourist:

Air Travel
The most convenient way to reach Jordan is by flying. The country is well-connected to major international cities, making it easily accessible for travelers. The principal entry point is Queen Alia International Airport, located near the capital city, Amman. Several major airlines offer regular flights to Amman from key cities across the globe. Additionally, visitors can also select other airports in Jordan, such as Aqaba or King Hussein International Airport, especially if their destination or itinerary is focused on the southern half of the country.

Visa Requirements
Before arranging your vacation, it's necessary to check the visa requirements for Jordan. Some nationalities may be eligible for visa-free entry or visa-on-arrival, while others would need to apply for a visa in advance through Jordanian embassies or online portals. Ensure you have all the appropriate documentation and comply with the visa restrictions to avoid any travel-related complications.

Land Crossings
If you are coming from nearby nations, such as Israel, Egypt, or Saudi Arabia, land crossings are an alternative. The most regularly used border crossings include the Allenby Bridge (King Hussein Bridge) from Israel, the Wadi Araba Border Crossing from Israel's southernmost city of Eilat, and the Arava Border Crossing from Aqaba, Jordan's harbor city.

Each border crossing has particular operation hours and visa restrictions, so investigate in beforehand and plan your route accordingly.

Sea Travel

For a unique experience, travelers can reach Jordan by water. Cruises and ferries operate in the Red Sea and the Gulf of Aqaba, linking Jordan to neighboring nations like Egypt and Saudi Arabia. Aqaba, Jordan's sole seaside city, serves as the principal entry point for sea visitors. Cruise guests often enjoy visa-free entrance when arriving in Jordan through scheduled shore excursions.

Internal Travel

Once you've landed in Jordan, navigating about the nation is very uncomplicated. Public transit, such as buses and minibusses, are available, linking major cities and settlements. Taxis are also a common means of travel, and Uber operates in Amman. However, if you desire more flexibility, try hiring a car. Road conditions are generally good, and driving allows you to explore off-the-beaten-path sites on your own time.

Domestic Flights

For vacationers with limited time or wanting to explore remote locations, domestic flights are available between Amman and Aqaba. These flights offer a time-efficient solution to travel the considerable distance between the northern and southern portions of Jordan.

Conclusion

Traveling to Jordan as a visitor is an adventure rich with historical discoveries, desert vistas, and pleasant encounters with the local culture. Whether you choose to fly directly to

Amman, pass a land border from a nearby nation, or explore the Red Sea by water, your travel to Jordan promises to be an exciting experience. Be careful to investigate visa regulations, transit options, and internal travel choices to make the most of your time in this fascinating country.

Top Attractions

Jordan is recognized for its rich history, cultural legacy, and magnificent landscapes. For travelers seeking an extraordinary vacation experience, Jordan provides a wealth of attractions that include ancient archaeological sites, bustling towns, and natural beauties. Here are the top attractions in Jordan:

Petra

Petra, sometimes referred to as the "Rose City," is a stunning archaeological monument located in southern Jordan. This UNESCO World Heritage Site is a masterpiece of ancient engineering, culture, and history that draws travelers from around the world.

Nestled within the steep highlands of southern Jordan, Petra was the capital of the Nabatean Kingdom, a trading center that flourished from roughly the 4th century BC to the 2nd century AD. The Nabateans, a nomadic Arab people, expertly carved their city into the rose-red cliffs of the region, producing elaborate tombs, temples, and other structures that served as both useful places and creative expressions.

The most prominent structure in Petra is the Treasury (Al-Khazneh), an extravagant mausoleum that welcomes tourists as they walk through the narrow Siq, a natural rock fissure that serves as the entrance to the city. The sight of the Treasury rising from the tiny route is a beautiful scene that has been recorded in numerous images and films. The elaborate sculptures and grandeur of the Treasury highlight the great craftsmanship of the Nabateans.

Beyond the Treasury, Petra's terrain is littered with many other outstanding monuments, such as the Monastery (Ad-Deir), a vast mausoleum with a similar façade to the Treasury but on an even larger scale. To reach the Monastery, travelers embark on a difficult uphill journey, rewarded with magnificent views of the surrounding region upon arrival.

The Royal Tombs, high up on the cliffs, offer greater insight into the Nabatean burial rituals and architectural prowess. The Urn Tomb, Palace Tomb, and Corinthian Tomb are among the most renowned. Each tomb exhibits elaborate carvings and architectural details that illustrate the Nabateans' ability to harmoniously combine their designs with the natural rock formations.

Petra's function as a trading hub is reflected in the remains of its colonnaded roadway, which was formerly lined with market booths, shops, and other commercial establishments. The Great Temple, an immense edifice that formerly stood at the center of the city, speaks to the spiritual and cultural life of the Nabateans.

Beyond the ancient wonders, Petra is placed in a unique desert landscape that adds to its attractiveness. The desert terrain is marked by high sandstone cliffs, colorful rock formations, and the rare verdant oasis. The mix between the natural surroundings and the man-made structures provides a bizarre and awe-inspiring experience for visitors.

To really appreciate the majesty of Petra, it's advised to spend at least a day touring the site. Guided tours are provided for individuals who want to delve into the historical and cultural significance of each structure. Additionally, there are nightly candlelight tours, where guests may observe the Treasury illuminated by hundreds of flickering candles, creating a magnificent environment.

Petra's popularity has grown significantly over the years, resulting in increased efforts in protecting and conserving the site. Sustainable tourist practices are urged to reduce the influence on the delicate rock-cut structures and the surrounding ecosystem.

Jerash

Amphitheater

The history of Jerash extends back to Greco-Roman antiquity, where it prospered as a significant center of trade and culture. The city's spectacular remains, expertly kept over centuries, stand as a tribute to its grandeur. The majestic Hadrian's Arch, built to honor Emperor Hadrian's visit, greets tourists at the entry and acts as a symbolic doorway into the past. As you step through, the main street, the Cardo Maximus, spreads ahead, lined with majestic columns, temples, and shops that were once bustling with activity. Walking along this ancient street, one can practically sense the echoes of the past, visualizing the vivid scenes that unfolded here centuries ago.

The Oval Forum, a large public square, stands as the center of Jerash. Imagine the place alive with gatherings, political conversations, and performances. Today, this same place offers cultural events and festivals, linking the ancient and contemporary features of the city. The South Theater, a huge amphitheater carved into the hillside, exhibits the Romans' architectural prowess and was utilized for numerous entertainment events. Today, it comes alive with music and theater performances during the Jerash Festival, a genuine celebration of the city's legacy.

Beyond the magnificent architecture, Jerash offers a peep into daily life with its well-preserved ruins. The Nymphaeum, a beautiful ornamental fountain, and the delightfully preserved buildings with their elaborate mosaics provide insights into the everyday routines and aesthetics of the city's occupants. The Jerash Archaeological Museum exhibits a collection of objects excavated from the site, offering light on the numerous eras that impacted Jerash's history.

While the past is certainly a hallmark of Jerash, the city is far from being trapped in history. Modern Jerash survives alongside its old remains, allowing tourists a chance to immerse themselves in local culture. Souqs (markets) bustle with activity, showcasing handicrafts, fabrics, and spices. Engaging with the locals, experiencing traditional foods, and purchasing unique souvenirs are experiences that complete the voyage through Jerash.

To properly enjoy the city's charm, arranging your visit to coincide with the annual Jerash Festival is highly suggested. This event transforms the ancient ruins into stages for live performances, including music, dance, and dramatic events. The forum, theaters, and other historical structures become locations for a cultural event that attracts both local and international visitors.

Amman

The capital city of Jordan is a remarkable location that perfectly integrates a strong historical past with modern metropolitan life. This bustling metropolis gives travelers a unique experience that encompasses old archaeological sites, vibrant markets, rich cuisine, and a warm blend of cultures.

With a history stretching back to the Bronze Age, Amman is a city steeped in antiquity. The Amman Citadel, perched atop a hill, stands as a tribute to the city's historical significance. The Citadel features relics from numerous civilizations, including Roman, Byzantine, and Umayyad, providing an architectural mosaic that spans millennia. One of the most outstanding structures within the Citadel is the Temple of Hercules, a Roman edifice featuring towering columns and elaborate decorations.

Amman's old center, colloquially known as the "Balad," is a labyrinth of small alleyways, bustling markets, and classic buildings. The lively souks offer a sensory assault of sights, sounds, and fragrances, where one may bargain for spices, fabrics, jewelry, and local handicrafts. Rainbow Street, packed with cafes, art galleries, and boutiques, gives a contemporary edge to the historical region.

The city's religious diversity is also an important component of its identity. The King Abdullah I Mosque, with its distinctive blue dome and remarkable grandeur, is an iconic landmark. Visitors can observe the mosque's beautiful Islamic architecture and tranquil interior. Additionally, the Coptic Orthodox Church and the Al-Husseini Mosque show the amicable coexistence of many faiths in Amman.

Amman's modernity is equally intriguing. As one of the most westernized cities in the region, it serves as a center of trade, technology, and education. The city's skyline is studded with elegant buildings, luxury hotels, and sophisticated shopping centers that house multinational brands. The juxtaposition of this contemporary infrastructure against the backdrop of old sites produces a compelling contrast that defines the city's unique identity.

Food connoisseurs will find themselves in gourmet bliss in Amman. The city offers a delightful selection of meals that reflect the region's gastronomic tradition. From the delicious flavors of falafel and shawarma to the aromatic spices of mansaf, a classic Jordanian dish, the local cuisine is a journey in itself. The city's multinational population has also contributed to a diversified food scene, with restaurants providing cuisines from throughout the world.

Madaba

Nestled in the heart of Jordan, the historic city of Madaba beckons travelers with its rich history, colorful culture, and breathtaking mosaic art. This fascinating site, frequently referred to as the "City of Mosaics," holds a crucial place in the tapestry of human civilization. With a history extending over millennia and a unique blend of influences, Madaba gives visitors a trip through time, art, and heritage.

Madaba claims a history that reaches back to the Bronze Age, making it one of the oldest continually inhabited cities in the world. Its strategic location along historic trade routes contributed to its growth, resulting in a melting pot of cultures and traditions. The city's historical significance is most famously tied to its role as a hub for Byzantine and early Christian populations. One of Madaba's crown jewels is the 6th-century mosaic map of Jerusalem and the Holy Land, preserved in the Greek Orthodox Church of St. George. This masterpiece is one of the oldest surviving portrayals of the Holy Land and provides vital insights into the topography and architecture of the time.

Madaba's title as the "City of Mosaics" is well-deserved. Its artisans have honed the craft of mosaic craftsmanship over the years. Mosaics are not only decorations; they are windows into the past. The mosaics seen throughout Madaba's ancient sites, churches, and museums are a witness to the meticulous artistry of the past. These mosaics represent scenes from daily life, religious traditions, and mythological tales, providing visitors with an insight into the beliefs and ideals of ancient civilizations.

The city's religious variety is another feature that adds to its attraction. Madaba is home to several religious sites, including Christian churches, mosques, and shrines. The Church of St. John the Baptist is another important religious attraction, featuring a captivating collection of mosaic artwork. Beyond Christianity, Madaba retains religious significance for Muslims, as it is believed to be the spot where Moses first viewed the Promised Land.

Exploring Madaba isn't just about digging into history; it's also about immersing oneself in the local culture. The city's lively marketplaces, unique handicrafts, and authentic cuisine provide visitors with a true Jordanian experience. Traditional souvenirs such as pottery, woven linens, and finely created jewelry exhibit the artistic talents of the local craftspeople.

While entrenched in history, Madaba has embraced modernity without compromising its identity. The city offers a choice of housing options to suit different budgets and preferences. Its central location in Jordan makes it an ideal base for exploring other surrounding sights including the Dead Sea, Mount Nebo, and Petra. The city's accessibility has been upgraded over the years, making it easier for travelers to experience its attractions.

Mount Nebo

Mount Nebo, an old landmark of historical and religious significance, sits towering in the heart of Jordan, overlooking the picturesque Jordan Valley, the Dead Sea, and even glimpses of Jerusalem on a clear day. This treasured location is intertwined with various levels of cultural, spiritual, and archaeological value.

Rising to an elevation of roughly 800 meters (2,600 feet) above sea level, Mount Nebo is often regarded as the spot where the Biblical figure Moses is claimed to have glimpsed the Promised Land before passing away. According to religious sources, it is atop this hill that Moses was offered a sight of the country that the Israelites would come to inhabit after their arduous journey through the wilderness. This dramatic occasion is honored through the Moses Memorial Church, a sanctuary that presently graces the mountaintop. The church's beautiful mosaics, some dating back to the 6th century, depict scenes from the Old Testament, delivering a strong visual representation of the area's sacred importance.

The historical and archaeological relevance of Mount Nebo is increased by the discovery of remnants from numerous periods of human occupancy. Ruins of Byzantine churches, monasteries, and even a small settlement have been found, attesting to the site's continued use over the years. These archaeological artifacts provide a unique window into the lives of ancient residents, revealing light on their architectural methods, daily routines, and spiritual customs.

For history aficionados, a visit to Mount Nebo Archaeological Park is a voyage into the past. The park has a variety of relics and exhibitions that dive into the history of the site, presenting a detailed account of its significance from prehistoric periods to the current day. The park also boasts breathtaking panoramic vistas that span across the Jordan Valley, providing visitors with a moment of introspection as they stand where Moses once stood, considering his crucial role in defining the narrative of the region.

Beyond its spiritual and historical relevance, Mount Nebo captivates nature enthusiasts with its beautiful scenery. The harsh terrain and distinctive flora and fauna of the area provide an extra dimension of fascination to the experience. Adventurous spirits can explore the trekking routes that wind through the neighboring hills, allowing a greater connection to the natural splendor that has welcomed this spot for millennia.

In terms of accessibility, Mount Nebo is easily placed within a short drive from Jordan's capital, Amman, making it a great day trip for vacationers. Whether you're a pilgrim seeking a connection to ancient spirituality, an archaeology geek wanting to unravel the layers of history, or a nature lover wishing for panoramic panoramas, Mount Nebo offers an experience that resonates on several levels.

Ajloun Castle

Ajloun Castle, also known as Qal'at Ar-Rabad, is a historical jewel hidden in the beautiful hills of northern Jordan. Perched atop Jabal Auf, a peak overlooking the town of Ajloun and the surrounding valleys, the fortress was completed in 1184 by the great Islamic general Salah ad-Din, popularly known as Saladin. Its strategic location was chosen to control and safeguard the iron mines in the area, which were important for producing weaponry. This stronghold played a key role in guarding against Crusader raids and preserving sovereignty over the region.

Ajloun Castle's architecture is a stunning combination of Islamic and Crusader influences. The facade boasts robust limestone walls, defensive towers, and battlements, showcasing the castle's military purpose. As you explore its well-preserved interior, you'll uncover a maze of passageways, chambers, and stairs that provide insight into the daily life of those who formerly lived in the castle.

One of the castle's most spectacular features is the center courtyard, flanked by arched galleries. This courtyard acted as a gathering place and gave access to various parts of the castle. The central keep, known as the donjon, gives spectacular panoramic views of the surrounding terrain, allowing visitors to appreciate the castle's strategic importance. From this vantage point, one can envisage the epic wars that transpired across the gorgeous terrain.

For history aficionados, Ajloun Castle presents a riveting narrative about the medieval period. The displays within the castle walls include informational panels and relics that throw light on the castle's construction, its significance in regional defense, and the architectural techniques adopted by its builders. Visitors can also learn about the interactions between many civilizations throughout this era, which left a lasting imprint on the castle's design and purpose.

The trip to Ajloun Castle is an experience in itself. The trip through the Jordanian countryside offers insights into local life and scenery, providing richness to your understanding of the region. Once you arrive, the castle's dominating presence and the peaceful beauty of its environs leave an indelible impact.

Exploring the castle is an engaging adventure. As you travel through its passageways and rooms, the cool stone walls provide relief from the surrounding heat, while the echoing whispers of history take you back in time. Visitors can partake in guided tours, where skilled guides illuminate the castle's history with tales of battles, monarchs, and daily life. These guides generally stress the castle's strategic significance in the greater context of the region's history.

In recent years, preservation measures have enhanced the castle's accessibility and safeguarded its longevity. Ajloun Castle is currently a protected historical landmark and a tribute to Jordan's commitment to preserving its cultural heritage.

Dana Biosphere Reserve

The Dana Biosphere Reserve is a rare natural gem located in southern Jordan, allowing travelers an unparalleled opportunity to enjoy the stunning beauty and richness of the region. Encompassing a large area of approximately 300 square kilometers, the reserve is a paradise for nature enthusiasts, adventure seekers, and those interested in cultural experiences.

Nestled within the Great Rift Valley, the reserve has a spectacular mix of landscapes, ranging from dramatic sandstone cliffs and deep valleys to broad desert plateaus and rocky outcrops. The diversified topography supports a vast spectrum of flora and animals, making it an ideal location for eco-tourism. As guests explore the reserve's trails, they can encounter rare plant species, interesting geological structures, and an astounding diversity of wildlife. From the elusive Nubian ibex to the majestic Griffon vulture, the reserve is home to several species that have adapted to the harsh desert climate.

One of the most famous attractions within the Dana Biosphere Reserve is the Feynan Ecolodge, a model of sustainable tourism. This eco-friendly lodge provides travelers with luxurious lodgings while minimizing its environmental impact. Visitors can join in activities such as guided walks, traditional cooking courses, and stargazing sessions, all while learning about the local Bedouin culture and its deep connection to nature. The lodge's commitment to sustainability resonates with the general concept of the reserve, which emphasizes the significance of maintaining natural resources for future generations.

For those seeking adventure, the Dana Biosphere Reserve provides a wealth of outdoor activities that suit varied levels of fitness and interests. Hiking is a particularly popular pastime, with routes leading through some of the reserve's most magnificent scenery. The Dana to Petra walk, for instance, offers intrepid guests a multi-day journey through gorges, wadis, and historic sites, concluding in the ancient city of Petra. This hike not only exhibits the reserve's natural beauty but also underlines its historical significance as part of the old Incense Route.

While the Dana Biosphere Reserve mostly draws nature enthusiasts, its cultural and historical value should not be neglected. The reserve is home to a multitude of archaeological monuments, including historic copper mines that stretch back thousands of years. Exploring these places provides an insight into the region's rich history and the manner in which its inhabitants have connected with the land throughout the millennia. Additionally, encounters with the

surrounding Bedouin communities allow travelers an
opportunity to learn about traditional lifestyles and customs
that have been perpetuated for generations.

Umm Qais

Nestled in the northern hills of Jordan, Umm Qais serves as a tribute to the rich history and cultural legacy of the region. This archaeological gem offers travelers a unique opportunity to trip back in time while enjoying the spectacular natural splendor that surrounds it.

Umm Qais, also known as Gadara in antiquity, was once a thriving Greco-Roman metropolis. Its advantageous location overlooking the Sea of Galilee, the Yarmouk River, and the Golan Heights made it a vital hub for trade and business. The city flourished under different civilizations, including the Greeks, Romans, and Byzantines. Today, Umm Qais shows the vestiges of these ancient civilizations through its well-preserved ruins.

One of the highlights of any visit to Umm Qais is the Roman Theater. Carved onto the hillside, this enormous amphitheater could seat thousands of spectators who came to enjoy theatrical performances and gladiatorial combat. As you sit in the aged stone seats, you can nearly hear the echoes of the past, envisioning the lively events that previously unfolded on this exact stage.

Walking through the Decumanus Maximus, the main street of the ancient city, tourists may observe the ruins of different structures that flanked the road. From the Nymphaeum, a monumental fountain covered with beautiful carvings, to the Basilica, a former marketplace and judicial center, the vestiges of Umm Qais' busy past exist at every step. The exquisite intricacies and architectural marvels stand as a tribute to the outstanding engineering skills of the time.

For history aficionados, the Umm Qais Museum is a treasure trove of items recovered from the site. Intricately carved statues, pottery, and mosaics reveal insights into the daily lives, beliefs, and artistic prowess of the people who once called this city home.

Beyond its historical significance, Umm Qais offers a visual treat that spans far beyond its archaeological treasures. Perched on a hill, the property affords panoramic views of the surrounding countryside. From this vantage point, tourists may observe the confluence of three countries: Jordan, Israel, and Syria. The vista of the Sea of Galilee shimmering in the background and the huge Yarmouk River valley below is nothing short of awe-inspiring. Sunset at Umm Qais is an especially magical event, as the warm hues of the sun's descent shed an ethereal glow over the ancient stones.

To enhance the experience, Umm Qais offers great cuisine alternatives. The village nearby, also named Umm Qais, features delightful restaurants providing traditional Jordanian food. Tourists can relish foods like Mansaf, Jordan's national dish, as well as numerous mezze choices. The warmth of the people gives an authentic touch to the overall experience.

Ma'in Hot Springs

Nestled in the heart of Jordan's rocky environment lies a hidden jewel that promises an unrivaled experience of relaxation and renewal - the Ma'in Hot Springs. This natural oasis, located about 58 kilometers southwest of the capital city of Amman, offers a unique blend of visual beauty and therapeutic benefits that have attracted tourists and locals alike for decades.

The Ma'in Hot Springs are a cluster of mineral-rich thermal springs that pour forth from the earth's depths, creating cascading waterfalls and pools of different temperatures. These springs are thought to have been used by ancient civilizations, including the Romans and Byzantines, for their claimed therapeutic abilities. Today, the springs are a popular destination for individuals looking to escape the hustle and bustle of everyday life and immerse themselves in the soothing embrace of nature.

Upon arrival, tourists are welcomed by a spectacular sight: cascades of boiling hot water that flow down the cliffs, meeting with colder streams below. The image itself is enough to inspire a sense of peace. The Ma'in Hot Springs resort has capitalized on this natural wonder, offering a range of opulent amenities that complement the therapeutic characteristics of the springs. From sophisticated spa treatments to thermal mineral pools, the resort provides a haven of tranquility where guests may repose in elegance.

The mineral makeup of the water is what truly sets Ma'in Hot Springs distinct. Rich in sulfur, magnesium, calcium, and other minerals, the springs are considered to give a variety of health benefits. The high sulfur concentration, for instance, is known to have anti-inflammatory and skin-soothing effects, making it a popular choice for individuals seeking treatment for illnesses such as arthritis and psoriasis. The therapeutic advantages of soaking in these mineral-rich waters are supplemented by the tranquil environment of the surroundings, producing an experience that benefits both body and mind.

For the adventurous-minded, the region surrounding the springs gives many opportunities for exploring. The Dead Sea, one of the saltiest pools of water on Earth, is just a short drive away. Floating effortlessly amid its buoyant seas is a unique and unforgettable experience. Additionally, the medieval city of Madaba noted for its stunning Byzantine mosaics, and the ancient rock-carved city of Petra, both within driving distance, provide for thrilling day outings from Ma'in.

The Ma'in Hot Springs also employ sustainable practices, harnessing the geothermal energy of the area to power the buildings and contribute to the preservation of the ecosystem. This commitment to eco-friendliness adds to the allure of the area for ethical guests who strive to minimize their ecological footprint.

Shobak Castle

Shobak Castle, also known as Montreal Castle, is a historically significant fortification located in the southern area of Jordan. This medieval fortification survives as a tribute to the rich history of the region. The castle's beginnings stretch back to the 12th century when it was constructed by the Crusaders, a group of European knights who attempted to establish their presence in the Holy Land. Shobak Castle was strategically positioned along a crucial trade route from Egypt to Syria, making it a vital bastion for both military and economic purposes. The castle was erected on a rocky slope, providing it with a magnificent view of the surrounding valleys and mountains, guaranteeing that any invading armies could be noticed from a distance.

The architecture of Shobak Castle exhibits a blend of European Crusader influences and local building traditions. The outside walls are marked by their large stone blocks, a feature prevalent in Crusader strongholds. However, the interior structures and layout display a combination of Crusader and Arabic design features, illustrating the exchanges between cultures during that period.

One of the most striking characteristics of Shobak Castle is its elaborate system of underground tunnels and cisterns. These subterranean corridors were built to store water and food supplies, guaranteeing that the castle could endure extended sieges. Exploring these tunnels provides tourists with a feeling of the inventiveness and engineering prowess of the people who erected the castle.

As history progressed, Shobak Castle changed hands several times. After its initial Crusader construction, it was later seized by the Ayyubid dynasty, a Muslim state founded by Saladin, the legendary fighter and leader who also played a vital part in the recovery of Jerusalem from the Crusaders. The castle continues to change between numerous kings and empires, each leaving its stamp on its construction and history.

Visitors at Shobak Castle can immerse themselves in a voyage through time as they explore amid the remains of turrets, battlements, and halls. The panoramic perspective from the castle's highest peaks offers a spectacular vista of the Jordanian terrain, allowing visitors to imagine the strategic importance of the castle once held. Exploring the ruins, one may envision the daily life of the people who lived within its walls and gain insight into the hardships they faced.

To make the most of a visit to Shobak Castle, it is important to wear comfortable footwear and take basics like water, sunscreen, and a hat, as the castle is situated in an arid region. Engaging the services of a professional guide can enhance the experience by providing historical context and entertaining anecdotes about the castle's past.

In recent years, the Jordanian government has undertaken measures to maintain and safeguard Shobak Castle, including restoration operations aimed at conserving its architectural integrity. This commitment to safeguarding cultural assets shows the castle's importance not only as a historical location but also as a symbol of the region's rich and interwoven past.

Baptism Site

The Baptism Site, also known as Bethany Beyond the Jordan, is a historically and spiritually significant location located in the Jordan Valley, near the eastern bank of the Jordan River. This landmark bears tremendous value for religious pilgrims, history aficionados, and tourists seeking a deeper knowledge of the region's cultural and spiritual past.

The Baptism Site is recognized as the location where, according to Christian tradition, Jesus Christ was baptized by John the Baptist. This occurrence is a key juncture in the life of Jesus, as it signifies his introduction into public ministry. For Christian pilgrims, visiting this site is equivalent to walking in the footsteps of Jesus and being part of a centuries-old ritual. The waters of the Jordan River, where the baptism is believed to have taken place, contain great spiritual value, and many visitors opt to engage in baptismal ceremonies as an act of faith and personal connection.

From an archaeological perspective, the Baptism Site has undergone significant excavations, uncovering ruins of churches, chapels, and baptismal pools going back to the Byzantine and Roman periods. These vestiges provide insights into the religious rituals and architectural styles of various eras, allowing visitors to imagine the places in which early Christians worshipped. The discoveries also contribute to the site's UNESCO World Heritage classification, drawing history enthusiasts who are captivated by the layers of civilization that have left their mark on the area.

The site's historical significance extends beyond its Christian associations. In the neighborhood of the Baptism Site, evidence supports the presence of an ancient settlement, which could be connected with the biblical "Bethany beyond the Jordan." This adds a dimension of curiosity for scientists and tourists interested in identifying the connections between archaeological findings and biblical tales.

As a visitor, a visit to the Baptism Site can be a multi-sensory experience. The tranquil surroundings, including the slowly flowing Jordan River and the desert environment, combine to a contemplative mood that invites introspection and spiritual connection. Many travel operators arrange guided tours that offer thorough explanations of the site's significance, historical context, and religious importance. These tours generally include visits to ancient sites, vantage places for breathtaking vistas, and chances for solo or group worship and reflection.

When arranging a vacation, it's recommended to consider the weather, as the Jordan Valley can endure intense temperatures throughout the summer months. Wearing adequate attire and staying hydrated is key for a good experience. Additionally, given the site's cultural and religious values, visitors are encouraged to show respect by adhering to clothing requirements and following norms for conduct.

Qasr al-Kharrana

Dating back to the early Umayyad period, which stretched from the 7th to 8th centuries CE, Qasr al-Kharrana was originally erected as a house for the ruling Umayyad aristocracy. Its unusual shape and strategic placement along old trade routes make it a fascinating representative of early Islamic architecture.

One of the most prominent elements of Qasr al-Kharrana is its unusual façade. The facade of the castle is covered with exquisite bas-relief decorations, exhibiting a blend of artistic elements from numerous cultures, including Byzantine, Persian, and Arab influences. These elaborate decorations not only served an aesthetic purpose but also showed the cosmopolitan nature of the Umayyad empire.

The castle's layout is similarly intriguing. Qasr al-Kharrana follows a rectangular plan, with a central courtyard surrounded by several apartments and hallways. This arrangement allowed for good climate control, with the courtyard functioning as a gathering area and the surrounding rooms giving respite from the harsh desert heat. The architects of the castle were conscious of the local environment, incorporating design aspects to enhance ventilation and cooling.

One of the castle's principal roles was to act as a waystation for travelers and traders navigating the dry regions of Jordan. The strategic location of Qasr al-Kharrana enables it to play a key role in promoting trade and communication between distant places. This is shown by its proximity to ancient trade routes that connected the Arabian Peninsula, Levant, and beyond.

For travelers, Qasr al-Kharrana offers a thrilling voyage into the past. Exploring the castle's interior shows a number of rooms that were formerly used as living quarters, storage places, and possibly administrative spaces. The architectural components, such as the finely designed entryway and windows, offer insight into the aesthetics and functional considerations of the time.

Beyond its architectural value, Qasr al-Kharrana also possesses cultural worth. It provides a tangible link to the Umayyad dynasty, allowing a look into the lives, social hierarchies, and technological developments of the period. This historical connection is further underlined by the continuous efforts to conserve and manage the place, ensuring that future generations can continue to appreciate its significance.

Visiting Qasr al-Kharrana demands an understanding of its setting within Jordan's broader historical and cultural landscape. Tourists have the possibility to combine their visit with investigations of other neighboring desert castles, each with its own unique characteristics and historical storylines. Additionally, the surrounding desert nature offers a magnificent backdrop for photography and times of introspection.

Azraq Wetland Reserve

One of the most noticeable features of the Azraq Wetland Reserve is its position as a major migratory stopover for various bird species. As a part of the East African-West Asian Flyway, it serves as a crucial resting and refueling site for millions of birds during their extended migrations between Europe, Asia, and Africa. The reserve's varied habitats, including pools, marshes, and mudflats, provide a diversified range of feeding and breeding possibilities for over 100 bird species. This makes it an incredible refuge for birdwatchers who can witness rare and endemic species, such as the globally threatened Basra Reed Warbler, along with various waterfowl, herons, and raptors.

But the Azraq Wetland Reserve is not just a sanctuary for birds; it also harbors a unique ecosystem adapted to the desert environment. Natural springs, known as "qanats," feed the marshes and create an atmosphere that is substantially cooler and more humid than its surroundings. This oasis-like habitat supports a mix of flora and animals, including reed beds, tamarisk trees, and desert-adapted fish like the famed Azraq Killifish, which is found nowhere else in the world.

The reserve also boasts historical significance. The ancient city of Azraq, which historically functioned as a key halt on trade routes, lies nearby. The Umayyad desert castle, erected in the 8th century, stands as a testimony to the area's historical importance. Visitors have the rare opportunity to explore the remnants of this castle and dig into the rich history that formed the region.

For eco-conscious travelers, the Azraq Wetland Reserve stands as a remarkable example of conservation initiatives in action. The Royal Society for the Conservation of Nature (RSCN) has been instrumental in maintaining this delicate habitat. Their projects focus on conserving the fragile balance of the wetlands while giving chances for sustainable tourism. Through guided tours and informative exhibits, visitors may learn about the challenges of desert conservation and observe the positive impact of responsible tourism.

A visit to the Azraq Wetland Reserve is an engaging experience that engages all the senses. The sights and sounds of the teeming birds, the soft rustling of the reeds, and the juxtaposition of brilliant hues against the desert landscape create an environment of peace and amazement. Guided tours conducted by the RSCN provide an in-depth overview of the reserve's ecological value and the ongoing efforts to maintain it.

Al-Karak

Nestled on a hill, Al-Karak boasts a commanding presence over the surrounding countryside. Its most famous landmark is the majestic Kerak Castle, a monument to the city's historical importance. This huge fortification is a superb example of Crusader architecture and goes back to the 12th century. Its massive walls, convoluted passageways, and strategic position make it an architectural marvel, presenting visitors with unique insights into the region's stormy past.

Walking through the small streets of Al-Karak, visitors may soak up the city's colorful atmosphere. The town is home to a varied community, integrating traditional Jordanian culture with modern influences. Local markets offer a chance to mingle with friendly sellers offering handicrafts, spices, and fabrics. Sampling local cuisine is a necessity – from the aromatic Mansaf, a typical Jordanian dish, to sweet sweets like Knafeh, the city's culinary culture is a pleasant exploration of flavors.

For history aficionados, Al-Karak is a rich trove of stories. The city's strategic placement along old trade routes has given rise to a rich past distinguished by many civilizations. Roman, Byzantine, and Islamic influences have all left their imprints on the city's architecture and culture. Exploring the Archaeological Museum provides a greater understanding of these influences, presenting objects that chart Al-Karak's history over the years.

The Dana Biosphere Reserve is close and offers nature lovers a chance to see Jordan's different ecosystems firsthand.

A short trek from Al-Karak leads to the awe-inspiring ancient city of Petra. The journey via the tiny Siq route, leading to the renowned Treasury building, is a truly unique experience.

To get the most out of a visit to Al-Karak, it's advisable to plan beforehand. The climate may be rather hot, especially during the summer months, so carrying suitable clothing and staying hydrated is crucial. Engaging a local guide can enhance the experience, as they can provide useful insights and tales about the city's history and culture.

Conclusion
Jordan's unique combination of historical significance, natural beauties, and friendly hospitality make it a particularly intriguing destination for travelers. Whether exploring ancient ruins, floating in the Dead Sea, or discovering the breathtaking landscapes of Wadi Rum, tourists to Jordan are bound to be fascinated by the country's treasures.

Top Cuisine to Try Out

Jordan cuisine shows a varied spectrum of flavors influenced by its geographic position and cultural background. A tourist visiting Jordan can go on a culinary adventure, discovering a diversity of foods that tickle the taste senses and leave a lasting impression. Here are some of the most popular foods in Jordan:

Mansaf

Mansaf is a savory dish typically made with lamb cooked in a special blend of spices, principally jameed (dried yogurt), which provides it with its distinctive sour flavor. The dish is often served on a huge communal platter over a bed of rice, which is typically fragrant and garnished with almonds and pine nuts, adding a lovely crunch to the dish. The entire platter is then usually offered atop a saj, a round flatbread that symbolizes Jordan's gracious hospitality.

But Mansaf is more than just a dish; it's an emblem of Jordanian culture and history. In Jordan, it's traditional to enjoy Mansaf with family and friends, frequently eaten without utensils as a gesture of solidarity and unity. The concept of eating from a shared plate shows the importance of social relationships in Jordanian society.

The meal is generally connected with festivals, gatherings, and special occasions, such as weddings or Eid al-Fitr. The manner Mansaf is cooked and savored represents the principles of charity, hospitality, and respect for traditions that are strongly established in Jordanian society. Tourists who join in a Mansaf feast get an intimate peek into the heart of Jordanian rituals and social dynamics.

For tourists, appreciating Mansaf is not just about relishing culinary mastery but also about embracing the culture that it represents. Many local eateries include Mansaf on their menus, typically offering guests a guided lesson on the dish's history and cultural significance. Engaging in talks with locals over a dish of Mansaf can lead to insights into daily life, traditions, and the warmth of Jordanian hospitality.

Falafel

Falafel's roots can be traced back to ancient Egypt when it was initially produced from fava beans. However, in Jordan, the original version is prepared with chickpeas, which gives it a distinct flavor and texture. The dish is thought to have been introduced to Jordan by the Palestinian and Egyptian groups that established in the region many decades ago.

Preparation of falafel in Jordan is an art form that takes talent and patience. The method begins by soaking dry chickpeas in water with a bit of baking soda, which helps to soften them. After several hours, the chickpeas are drained and mixed with aromatic spices such as cumin, coriander, and garlic, along with fresh herbs like parsley and cilantro. The mixture is then coarsely crushed to make a thick paste.

The following stage includes molding the falafel mixture into small balls or patties, generally with the aid of a falafel scoop or bare hands. These falafel balls are deep-fried until they attain a crispy, golden-brown outside while preserving a tender, delicious interior. The final result is a delicious combination of textures that leaves the taste receptors begging for more.

In Jordan, falafel is often prepared in a number of ways, catering to diverse tastes and preferences. One of the most popular options is as a filling for pita bread, combined with a medley of fresh veggies like lettuce, tomatoes, cucumbers, and sour pickles. The sandwich is sometimes paired with creamy tahini sauce, giving a rich, nutty flavor to the ensemble. Some cafés also offer falafel prepared on a plate, accompanied by an array of delectable dips including hummus, baba ganoush, and tabbouleh.

Beyond its wonderful taste, falafel carries cultural significance in Jordan. It is seen as a symbol of unification, bringing people from all backgrounds together to share this cherished street dish. Throughout Jordanian cities, bustling falafel shops and restaurants are a familiar sight, offering locals and tourists alike an opportunity to unite over shared culinary pleasures.

Moreover, falafel has a historical relationship with the region's agricultural legacy. Chickpeas, a crucial ingredient in falafel, have been farmed in the Middle East for thousands of years. Thus, consuming falafel in Jordan is not simply a culinary delight but also a means to connect with the country's agricultural past.

For travelers seeking a real falafel experience, there are various places that have become recognized for their superb preparation of this favorite food. One may venture to Hashem

Restaurant in downtown Amman, a long-standing business liked by locals and expats alike. Alternatively, the lively lanes of Al-Balad in Amman are packed with falafel vendors, each offering their unique variation on the traditional.

Hummus

Hummus, pronounced "hoo-moos," originates from ancient Egypt, but it has been embraced and altered by numerous Middle Eastern countries, including Jordan. It is a creamy, savory spread made mostly from cooked and mashed chickpeas combined with tahini (ground sesame paste), olive oil, lemon juice, garlic, and a bit of salt. These ingredients beautifully mix to create a velvety texture and a distinctive, zesty flavor that thrills the palate.

Jordanian hummus distinguishes out due to the superior quality of its locally sourced ingredients, skillfully prepared by experienced chefs and home cooks alike. Chickpeas are soaked and cooked until tender, allowing them to acquire the right consistency. Tahini, commonly made from Jordan's rich sesame seeds, adds depth and smoothness, while the use of locally produced olive oil enriches the nutty overtones. Lemon juice gives a refreshing taste, while the garlic infuses the spread with a wonderful spice.

The presentation of hummus in Jordan is an art form. It is traditionally served on a shallow platter, with a central well for olive oil and sometimes extra toppings such as whole chickpeas, parsley, paprika, or sumac. Accompanied by freshly made pita bread or crisp veggies, the dish enables diners to shred and scoop, experiencing the communal and interactive dining experience.

Beyond its gastronomic value, hummus reflects a cultural and social aspect in Jordan. Sharing hummus among friends and family during gatherings is a valued ritual, generating a sense of togetherness and warmth. In restaurants, street-side cafes, and even homes, hummus serves as a unifying meal, bringing people together to savor and celebrate their shared heritage.

As a tourist, exploring hummus in Jordan means immersing oneself in the core of its culture and culinary habits. By visiting local cafes and marketplaces, one may watch the cooking process firsthand and receive insight into the passion and pride that go into preparing this famous food. Engaging with locals also offers an opportunity to learn about the customs and tales around hummus, adding complexity to the culinary trip.

Shawarma

Shawarma consists of succulent marinated meat, often chicken, lamb, or beef, slowly roasted on a vertical rotisserie. The meat is seasoned with a medley of spices including cumin, coriander, paprika, and garlic, infusing it with an appealing aroma and soft texture. Each Shawarma vendor has their proprietary blend, providing a unique touch to the dish.

When a tourist orders Shawarma in Jordan, the show begins. The talented cook skillfully carves the delicious meat off the spinning spit, and elegantly wraps it on a thin, soft flatbread known as "pita." The meat is accompanied by an array of toppings like freshly chopped parsley, pungent pickles, crunchy cucumbers, sliced tomatoes, and a drizzle of creamy tahini or garlic sauce.

Beyond the amazing mix of ingredients, Shawarma is a culinary marvel rooted in history. Its roots may be traced back to the Ottoman Empire and the Levant region, making it a culinary symbol of cultural exchange and history. While the meal has evolved over time, its essence remains intact, a tribute to the lasting effect of cuisine in molding a nation's identity.

For tourists, Shawarma acts as a cultural gateway, expressing the friendliness and openness of the Jordanian people. This beloved street cuisine may be found at bustling markets, busy street corners, and even in small wayside booths. The community experience of waiting in line with locals and sharing the thrill of indulging in this wonderful dessert produces an unforgettable memory for any visitor.

Moreover, Shawarma is not just a meal; it's a social activity. Jordanians commonly congregate with friends and family to share Shawarma, generating a sense of friendship and solidarity. It's not uncommon to observe residents engaged in conversation, animatedly discussing their day over a plate of Shawarma.

Kebabs

The kebab, called locally "meshawi," represents a beloved custom passed down through generations. Jordanian cuisine derives inspiration from the region's unique past, which includes Bedouin, Palestinian, and Arabian culinary cultures. These varied influences combine perfectly in the kebab, creating a dish that says much about the country's cultural tapestry.

At its foundation, the kebab consists of juicy pieces of marinated meat, frequently lamb or chicken, artfully skewered and grilled to perfection over open flames. The technique of marinating the meat resides in the balance of spices, such as cumin, sumac, and a touch of lemon, which infuse the kebab with an appealing aroma and flavor. This thorough preparation guarantees that each kebab is a gourmet treat that symbolizes the pride and craftsmanship of Jordanian chefs.

The kebab experience is more than simply a meal; it's an invitation to connect with Jordanian culture. Many Jordanians take enormous delight in sharing their love for kebabs, and communal gatherings often center around this exquisite delicacy. Whether savored in a noisy restaurant, a local diner, or at a boisterous outdoor barbeque, the act of eating kebabs produces a sense of camaraderie and conviviality that encapsulates the essence of Jordanian hospitality.

One cannot completely appreciate kebabs in Jordan without investigating the multitude of variants offered. Each location claims its own unique spin on the meal, from the succulent Shish Taouk in Amman to the earthy and aromatic Zarb prepared in the desert sands of Wadi Rum. These geographical variances highlight how the kebab has adapted and evolved within Jordanian culture, engaging with both locals and visitors alike.

For tourists seeking a thorough understanding of kebabs in Jordan, traveling to local markets is vital. Souqs like the busy Al Balad in Amman offer an immersive experience where tourists may watch the diversity of spices, fresh ingredients, and skillful sellers who contribute to the kebab's preparation. Engaging with people and learning about the cooking processes is an enriching encounter that enriches one's awareness of Jordanian food.

Maqluba

Translated as "upside-down" in Arabic, Maqluba exhibits a visually pleasing arrangement of meat, rice, and vegetables cooked in a single pot before being flipped upside-down for serving. Beyond its culinary appeal, Maqluba has become a symbol of hospitality and togetherness, embodying the essence of Jordanian culture.

The production of Maqluba is a labor of love, generally needing hours of cooking to acquire its particular flavor. Cooks start by sautéing meat, generally chicken, lamb, or beef, along with onions and a combination of spices until it reaches a luscious and tender texture. They next cover the half-cooked beef with vegetables, such as eggplants, potatoes, tomatoes, and cauliflower. The final layer consists of long-grain rice, soaked previously to promote equal cooking. As the pot simmers, the flavors meld together, creating a perfect combination that makes Maqluba a treat for the taste senses.

Beyond its culinary benefits, Maqluba has deep-rooted cultural importance. It is commonly cooked for important occasions and family gatherings, reflecting generosity and warmth. The act of tipping the pot upside-down onto a big serving platter demands talent and coordination, frequently leading to a communal ovation and jubilant celebrations, making it a highlight of any occasion. The meal is served with sides of yogurt or salad, thus complementing the overall dining experience.

For tourists visiting Jordan, Maqluba offers a unique opportunity to immerse themselves in the local culture and traditional food. Many restaurants across the country serve this dish, and it is also usual to be welcomed to a Jordanian house to join in this communal feast. Sharing Maqluba with locals builds an intimate relationship with Jordanian hospitality, delivering a glimpse into the warmth and unity loved by its people.

Maqluba also delivers a nutritious and balanced supper. The combination of meat, veggies, and rice provides important nutrients, and the absence of heavy sauces or excessive oil makes it a healthier alternative compared to many other traditional dishes.

As with any cultural activity, it is crucial for tourists to approach Maqluba with respect and admiration for the traditions it represents. Engaging in the making and sharing of this renowned dish builds cross-cultural understanding and strengthens bridges between tourists and local communities.

Warak Enab

Warak Enab, also known as Stuffed Grape Leaves, is a cuisine that revolves around grape leaves, which are painstakingly plucked and kept in a brine solution to keep them fresh. The leaves are then stuffed with a wonderful mixture of rice, ground meat (typically lamb or beef), tomatoes, onions, garlic, and a blend of aromatic herbs and spices, such as parsley, mint, allspice, and cinnamon. The stuffing is a crucial aspect of the recipe, as it contributes to the dish's characteristic taste and character.

To produce Warak Enab, the stuffed grape leaves are precisely wrapped into tight bundles and gently baked. Traditionally, the rolls are cooked in a pot with a layer of lamb bones or chicken pieces at the bottom to infuse the meal with additional flavors. Lemon juice and olive oil are often sprinkled over the grape leaves during cooking, increasing the overall taste.

Warak Enab possesses cultural significance in Jordan and the greater Middle Eastern region. It is typically offered during family reunions, weddings, and special occasions, reflecting warmth, hospitality, and generosity. The dish's preparation frequently requires a collective effort among family members, establishing ties and sustaining cultural traditions.

As a tourist, trying Warak Enab provides an opportunity to appreciate the original flavors of Jordanian cuisine and experience the country's culinary legacy firsthand. Many local restaurants and food booths provide this meal, making it readily available to tourists.

Beyond the wonderful taste, Warak Enab also offers insight into the region's farming techniques. The use of grape leaves in cooking reflects the significance of grape production in Jordan, which has a long history of winemaking reaching back to ancient times.

Knafeh

Knafeh, also known as kuna fa, is a scrumptious and legendary dessert in Jordan that has achieved tremendous appeal among locals and visitors alike. Originating from the city of Nablus in Palestine, Knafeh is a sweet pastry prepared with layers of shredded phyllo dough, a substantial filling of sweet cheese, and a drizzle of sugar-based syrup that gives it a delightful sweetness. The mixture is then roasted in an oven until it turns golden brown, creating a wonderful balance of textures and flavors that are absolutely tempting.

To feel the true flavor of Knafeh in Jordan, one must wander into the lively marketplaces and local bakeries that dot the streets. These establishments take pleasure in making this wonderful dish, with many using age-old recipes passed down through generations. Some of the best-known venues to try Knafeh in Jordan include Al-Nabulsi Sweets and Habibah Sweets in the capital city, Amman.

What sets Jordanian Knafeh apart is the particular use of a rare cheese called Nabulsi, giving it a unique taste that is acidic and sweet simultaneously. The contrast between the crunchy crust and the creamy cheese interior produces a delicious experience that leaves a lasting impression.

Knafeh is not simply a dessert but also a symbol of Jordanian hospitality and kindness. It is typically served at festive events, family gatherings, and during the holy month of Ramadan, where its exquisite taste improves the sense of unity and communal joy.

Beyond its flavor and cultural significance, Knafeh reflects the kindness of Jordanian society, as locals willingly share their favorite sites to eat this delicacy. Visitors can engage with the friendly inhabitants, getting insights into the traditions and practices related to Knafeh, while savoring every bite.

For travelers with dietary restrictions, certain bakeries have started creating unique varieties of Knafeh, catering to diverse preferences and guaranteeing that everyone may experience this renowned pleasure.

Mutabbaq

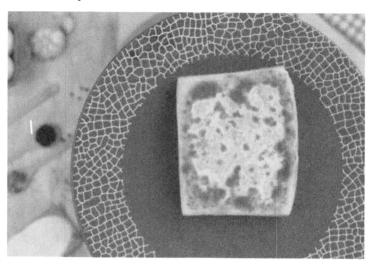

This popular street dish is a delightful pastry famed for its savory and spiced ingredients, wrapped in a thin, flaky dough and then deep-fried to golden perfection. Its history can be traced back to the Bedouin tribes, who invented it as a portable meal for their wandering lifestyle.

The name "mutabbaq" is derived from the Arabic word "tabbāq," meaning "folded." Indeed, the production of mutabbaq entails folding the dough over the filling, sealing the edges, and making a triangular or rectangular shape. The fillings vary greatly, displaying the richness of Jordanian cuisine. Among the most typical fillings are spiced ground beef, onions, and sometimes vegetables, offering a delicious and substantial taste.

To properly sample the original flavors of mutabbaq, travelers should visit crowded marketplaces and street vendors throughout Jordan. In Amman's center, the Rainbow Street neighborhood and the famed Hashem Restaurant are great sites to sample this delicacy. The tempting fragrance of freshly fried mutabbaq would persuade every onlooker to indulge in this gourmet pleasure.

Each location in Jordan has its own distinct take on mutabbaq. For instance, in the city of Karak, you may discover the "Karak mutabbaq," often packed with a blend of spiced beef, onions, and aromatic herbs. In Petra, a tourism destination, the filling may use local ingredients like goat cheese or za'atar, a savory herb blend.

The preparation method is an art in itself, handed down through generations. Vendors carefully blend the spices to enhance the flavors without dominating the delicate taste of the dough. Observing the cooks carefully make these triangular delicacies adds to the charm of the event.

Besides being a gourmet delight, mutabbaq signifies Jordan's rich cultural legacy and communal spirit. It acts as a symbol of unity, bringing together locals and tourists alike. Sharing a hot and freshly prepared mutabbaq with friends or strangers develops a sense of solidarity, bridging language barriers and cultural divides.

Jordanian Salad

Salad and Kebab

Jordanian Salad, also known as Salata Baladi, is a simple yet delicious blend of fresh and locally obtained ingredients, reflecting the country's devotion to using the finest products available. The core of this salad is made up of crisp cucumbers, ripe tomatoes, and tangy onions, all precisely chopped to produce a harmonic mix of colors and textures. The vegetables are often diced or sliced into little, bite-sized pieces, making it simple to taste each delectable component.

What distinguishes Jordanian Salad distinct is its flavor and dressing. Generously drizzled with extra-virgin olive oil, a mainstay of Jordanian cuisine, the salad offers a deep and smooth taste that highlights the freshness of the veggies. Additionally, the generous use of lemon juice adds a tangy tang, creating a burst of flavor that balances the components wonderfully.

96

For the finishing touch, a dusting of sumac lends a distinct Middle Eastern twist. This dark red spice is derived from the dried berries of the sumac shrub, delivering a tart, somewhat lemony taste that enriches the whole salad experience. Some varieties of the meal may also contain mint leaves or parsley, providing a pleasant herbal touch to the combination.

Beyond its exquisite taste, Salata Baladi carries cultural value. It is commonly served during family gatherings, celebrations, and special occasions. The salad's presence on the table denotes hospitality and displays the warmth of Jordanian culture. As tourists enjoy this cuisine, they are welcomed into the heart of Jordan's culinary tradition, interacting with the local people and their way of life.

Moreover, the salad's simplicity and nutritious ingredients resonate with Jordan's commitment to natural and healthful eating. Many of the ingredients may be obtained in the country's plentiful markets and are sourced locally, supporting the region's agricultural community.

For tourists, tasting Salata Baladi provides a unique glimpse into Jordan's rich history and culinary traditions. The meal highlights the country's ability to integrate ingredients from the Mediterranean, Levantine, and Arabian cuisines, culminating in a gourmet treat that encapsulates the essence of the region.

When visiting Jordan, travelers can get this salad at numerous establishments, from high-end restaurants to simple street food vendors. Each chef may add their particular touch, making every plate a special experience. Sharing a plate of Salata Baladi with locals allows travelers a chance to engage on a deeper level, forging wonderful memories.

Conclusion

A gastronomic journey in Jordan offers travelers an opportunity to enjoy a delicious blend of textures and tastes strongly steeped in tradition and culture. From robust delicacies like Mansaf to the light and refreshing Mezze selections, every meal is an opportunity to interact with Jordan's rich heritage and welcoming hospitality. Whether you're roaming through lively markets or dining with locals in their homes, Jordan's cuisine promises an amazing experience for every food connoisseur.

Best Time To Visit

To truly experience the best of what Jordan has to offer, understanding the perfect time to come is vital. The optimum time to explore this gem of the Middle East depends on various aspects, like as weather, significant events, and personal preferences.

The climate in Jordan is generally dry and arid, with temperatures fluctuating greatly throughout the year. Generally, the most opportune time to visit is during the spring and fall months, from March to May and September to November, respectively. During these seasons, the weather is pleasantly mild, with temperatures ranging from 18 to 28 degrees Celsius, making outdoor activities fun and comfortable.

Springtime is particularly gorgeous as the landscapes come to life with brilliant blooms and lush foliage. This season is great for touring famous archaeological sites, including the UNESCO World Heritage site of Petra, where the temperature is neither too hot nor too cold, allowing tourists to fully immerse themselves in the glories of the ancient city.

Autumn is another wonderful time to visit Jordan. As the summer heat starts to wane, travelers can take advantage of cooler temperatures while still enjoying lengthy daytime hours for sightseeing. The famed desert of Wadi Rum is particularly attractive during this time, as the temperatures are more comfortable for desert activities and camping experiences beneath the stars.

For travelers hoping to dodge the crowds and secure cheaper rates, the shoulder seasons of late spring and early autumn are ideal alternatives. During certain months, tourist numbers are fewer, giving for a more intimate and quiet experience of the country's attractions. Additionally, lodging and trip prices tend to be more budget-friendly.

However, it's crucial to mention that the summer months, particularly June to August, should be tackled with caution due to blazing temperatures that can rise well above 35 degrees Celsius. Visiting during this time can be tough for outdoor activities, especially in desert regions. Nonetheless, if you can handle the heat, this is when you may explore some off-the-beaten-path sites and discover a quieter side of Jordan.

Winter, from December through February, is considered the low season in Jordan. While the weather is cooler, with daytime temperatures about 12 to 15 degrees Celsius, it's often more comfortable than the searing summer heat. This is a good time for history enthusiasts and those interested in ancient ruins to explore the historical sites without the crowds.

Moreover, if you're a fan of unusual cultural experiences, try planning your visit during notable events or festivals. For example, the Jordanian Jerash Festival takes place in July and highlights local and international acts, providing a beautiful insight into Jordanian arts and traditions.

Conclusion
The best time to visit Jordan mostly relies on personal interests and what you wish to experience. Spring and autumn are often preferred for good weather and ideal touring conditions. However, if you're prepared for the heat or want a

quieter experience, summer and winter can also provide unique options. Whichever period you select, Jordan's historical treasures, welcoming culture, and magnificent landscapes will definitely leave a lasting effect on every traveler.

Traveling Itinerary

A 1 to 2-week holiday in Jordan allows travelers to explore its historical treasures, see the marvels of the desert, float in the Dead Sea, and immerse themselves in the lively culture. Let's break down the itinerary for each week.

1-Week Vacation Itinerary

Day 1: Arrival in Amman
Upon arrival in Amman, the capital city of Jordan, take some time to recover and adjust to the new surroundings. Consider visiting the Amman Citadel, an important historical monument that gives panoramic views of the city.

Day 2: Jerash and Ajloun Castle
Embark on a day trip to Jerash, one of the best-preserved Roman cities in the world. Explore the well-preserved ruins, including the Temple of Artemis and the Oval Plaza. Continue to Ajloun Castle, a 12th-century castle with beautiful views of the surrounding area.

Day 3: Petra
Travel south to the ancient city of Petra, one of the New Seven Wonders of the World. Spend the day exploring the unique rock-cut buildings, including the renowned Treasury, the Monastery, and the Siq. Prepare for a spectacular night by participating in the Petra by Night event.

Day 4: Wadi Rum
Head to Wadi Rum's spectacular desert area known as the Valley of the Moon. Enjoy a 4x4 jeep drive to discover the

fascinating sand dunes, rock formations, and ancient inscriptions. Spend the night in a genuine Bedouin camp under the sky.

Day 5: Aqaba
Travel to Aqaba on the Red Sea shore, where you may enjoy aquatic sports like snorkeling or scuba diving. Relax on the gorgeous beaches or tour Aqaba's attractive city center.

Day 6: Dead Sea
Drive to the Dead Sea, the lowest location on Earth. Experience the unusual buoyancy of its salt-rich waters and indulge in a mud bath. Relax at one of the beautiful resorts along the Dead Sea beachfront.

Day 7: Departure from Amman
Return to Amman for departure, carrying with you memorable memories of Jordan's rich history and magnificent landscapes.

2-Week Vacation Itinerary

Days 1-7: Follow the 1-week itinerary as described above.

Day 8: Dana Biosphere Reserve
Visit Dana Biosphere Reserve, a refuge for animal and plant diversity. Enjoy trekking routes that offer spectacular views of the valley, and immerse yourself in the native Bedouin culture.

Day 9-10: Explore the Desert Castles
Embark on a two-day excursion to explore Jordan's Desert Castles, strewn across the eastern desert. These well-preserved castles and caravanserais display the architectural marvels of the Umayyad period.

Day 11-12: Madaba and Mount Nebo

Visit the town of Madaba, noted for its mosaic art. Explore the Madaba Archaeological Park and the Greek Orthodox Church of St. George, home to the famed Madaba Map. Continue to Mount Nebo, where Moses is claimed to have viewed the Promised Land.

Day 13-14: Amman and Departure

Return to Amman and spend the final days touring the city's vibrant souks, museums, and modern landmarks. Discover the local food and browse for unique handicrafts. Depart with a heart full of fond memories and a stronger appreciation of Jordan's rich cultural history.

Conclusion

Jordan's 1 and 2-week vacation itineraries offer a lovely blend of history, nature, and adventure. From the ancient treasures of Petra to the unearthly landscapes of Wadi Rum and the healing waters of the Dead Sea, Jordan promises a voyage of a lifetime for any traveler seeking a unique and enlightening experience.

Visiting On a Budget

While it may seem overwhelming to travel as a tourist on a budget, with some careful planning and insider suggestions, seeing Jordan's beauties without breaking the bank is entirely achievable. From old historic sites to magnificent landscapes, let's examine how you might enjoy a rewarding and cheap journey through this interesting nation.

First and foremost, time is essential. Avoid high tourist seasons, usually from April to May and September to October when costs tend to increase. Opt for off-peak months, such as November to March, for more reasonable rates on accommodations, tours, and activities.

Arriving at the capital, Amman will be your entry to Jordan's historical beauties. Accommodation options range from budget-friendly hostels to inexpensive hotels. Look for centrally placed places with adequate public transport connections to economize on transportation expenditures.

Exploring Amman's sights doesn't have to be pricey. Visit attractions like the Citadel and Roman Theater for a minimal entrance fee and meander through the bustling souks for a real local experience. Try typical street cuisine, such as falafel and shawarma, which are not only excellent but also budget-friendly.

A must-visit attraction in Jordan is the ancient city of Petra. Purchase a Jordan Pass in advance, which includes the visa price and access to Petra and many other attractions. Spend a whole day touring this UNESCO World Heritage site, marveling at the amazing rock-cut architecture of the Treasury, Monastery, and other monuments.

When traveling to the Wadi Rum desert, book a budget-friendly desert camp or opt for a day tour rather than an overnight stay to save on expenditures. Enjoy a jeep tour across the stunning desert scenery and learn about the Bedouin culture from local guides.

For water fans, the Dead Sea offers a unique and revitalizing experience. Consider visiting free public beaches or negotiating with hotels for a day permit to utilize their private facilities without staying overnight.

Traveling about the country is reasonably economical via public transportation, particularly the JETT Buses, which connect key tourist spots including Amman, Petra, and Aqaba. Alternatively, shared taxis or "service" cabs are a typical means of transportation for locals and can be a cost-effective way to get around.

Sampling local cuisine is a highlight of any visit to Jordan. Seek out local eateries and street sellers for traditional meals at moderate costs. Mezze platters, mansaf, and knafeh are just a few must-try foods that won't break the bank.

Aqaba, Jordan's sole beachfront city, gives the option to unwind by the Red Sea without overpaying for pricey resorts. Snorkeling and diving options are plentiful, and you can find reasonably priced water sports with local operators.

When planning your trip, be aware of spending on bottled water by carrying a reusable water bottle and refilling it at public fountains or restaurants. Additionally, haggling at markets and souvenir shops is a typical habit in Jordan, so don't hesitate to negotiate for better rates.

Conclusion

Visiting Jordan on a budget is an enriching and wonderful experience. By timing your vacation wisely, selecting reasonable hotels, getting a Jordan Pass, taking public transportation, relishing local cuisine, and being mindful of expenses, you may witness the delights of Jordan without hurting your budget. Embrace the cultural treasures, architectural marvels, and breathtaking landscapes that this ancient land has to offer, and make cherished experiences that will last a lifetime.

Getting Around

Getting around Jordan may be an amazing experience for travelers eager to explore this gorgeous and historically rich country. To make the most of your visit, recognizing the numerous transit alternatives and logistical issues is crucial.

Public Transportation
Jordan's public transportation system contains buses and minibusses, usually known as "Service Taxis" or "Jett Buses." These solutions are economical and connect most cities and towns across the country. They might not be the most comfortable, but they give an authentic experience and a chance to engage with locals.

Renting a Car
Renting a car is a popular choice for travelers who wish to discover Jordan at their own speed. Several foreign automobile rental firms operate in the major cities, and driving is reasonably uncomplicated, however, it's vital to exercise caution owing to variable road conditions.

Private Drivers and Taxis
For a more personalized and comfortable manner of traveling around, hiring a private driver or cab is an alternative. Negotiating the fare upfront is vital to avoid any misunderstandings.

Trains
Currently, Jordan has a modest railway system, with the main line extending from Amman to the city of Ma'an. While the rail service is not as broad as other transportation options, it can be a unique experience for travelers interested in train travel.

Shared Taxis

Shared taxis, called "servees," are a typical sight in Jordanian cities. These are shared with other passengers traveling in the same direction and offer a flexible and cost-effective means of transportation.

Local Transportation in Petra and Wadi Rum

Within the historic city of Petra and the wide desert of Wadi Rum, walking is the major means of transportation. Be prepared for long walks and ensure you have appropriate footwear.

Conclusion

Getting about Jordan takes careful preparation and analysis of the available transportation alternatives. Each form of transportation has its pros and limitations, so travelers should choose what best meets their interests and budget. Whether it's visiting the bustling streets of Amman, marveling at the ancient wonders of Petra, or experiencing the peacefulness of the Dead Sea, Jordan promises an amazing experience rich with history, culture, and natural beauty.

Shopping for Souvenirs

Apart from its historical landmarks and natural beauty, shopping for souvenirs in Jordan is a joyful endeavor that allows travelers to take a bit of the country's rich culture and tradition back home. From traditional handicrafts to fine jewelry, Jordan offers a varied choice of souvenirs to choose from, making it a shopper's delight.

One of the most sought-after souvenirs in Jordan is the traditional Bedouin handicrafts. The Bedouins, nomadic tribes with a deep-rooted tradition in the region, create exquisite and elaborate handmade goods. These crafts include colorful fabrics like carpets, rugs, and woven shawls, embellished with vibrant geometric patterns and symbolic themes. The art of weaving has been passed down through centuries, and these textiles are not only a monument to the Bedouins' artistic skills but also represent the rich cultural legacy of Jordan.

Another popular souvenir choice is the beautiful ceramics and pottery made by talented artists. The city of Madaba is renowned for its mosaic art, and visitors can find stunning mosaic pieces representing biblical scenes or geometric designs. Furthermore, pottery products like vases, plates, and bowls are often hand-painted with traditional themes, making them unique and beloved memories for travelers.

For those interested in traditional clothes, the vivid Bedouin costumes and keffiyehs, the characteristic red and white checkered headscarves, make for fantastic mementos. Wearing these traditional clothing provides an insight into the Bedouin way of life and pays honor to the region's cultural history. Visitors can purchase these apparel items in local markets and specialty shops throughout Jordan.

Jordan is also noted for its unusual jewelry. Bedouin silver jewelry, with beautiful filigree work, is highly treasured by both residents and visitors alike. Necklaces, bracelets, and rings with traditional designs retain cultural importance and are considered to offer good luck and protection. Many jewelry stores in large cities like Amman and Petra provide a broad assortment of these gorgeous items, making it easy for tourists to locate the right remembrance.

Of course, no talk on shopping for souvenirs in Jordan would be complete without discussing the world-famous Dead Sea items. The Dead Sea, with its mineral-rich waters, offers a choice of natural cosmetic products that are a favorite among travelers. From skincare needs like mud masks and salt scrubs to cosmetic products like soaps and creams, these items make for fantastic gifts and mementos.

Jordan's lively markets, known as souks, are where travelers can delight in a sensory overload of sights, sounds, and smells. The most notable among them is the souk in Amman, which has a large assortment of traditional items. Visitors can immerse themselves in the bustling atmosphere and haggle for unique mementos like as spices, herbs, and Jordanian delicacies like olive oil, honey, and dates. Exploring the souks is a must-do experience for every visitor wishing to experience the true Jordanian way of life.

Moreover, Petra also offers an exquisite shopping experience. The souvenir shops here include Bedouin crafts, delicate jewelry, and tiny reproductions of the renowned Treasury and other monuments. Shopping in Petra allows travelers to take a piece of this ancient wonder home with them, serving as a cherished remembrance of their visit.

For those interested in modern shopping experiences, Jordan's malls and boutiques add a contemporary twist to the souvenir hunt. Amman's modern retail districts like Rainbow Street and Al Abdali Boulevard provide a mix of high-end businesses and local boutiques, making it a great destination for fashion-conscious tourists seeking fashionable souvenirs.

Conclusion
Shopping for souvenirs in Jordan is an immersive experience that reflects the country's rich cultural heritage. From traditional Bedouin handicrafts and vivid textiles to elaborate jewelry and Dead Sea goods, tourists are spoilt for choice. Exploring the colorful souks and sophisticated retail districts provides an amazing shopping experience, enabling visitors to take a piece of Jordan's magic back home with them. As a monument to its cultural richness, buying souvenirs in Jordan is not just about getting mementos but also about generating lasting memories of a truly exceptional vacation.

Tour Package Options

A tourist's journey through this interesting country can be made all the more delightful and hassle-free with well-designed tour packages that cater to a variety of interests and preferences.

Historical Tours: For history aficionados, Jordan's rich past offers a treasure trove of experiences. Tour packages commonly include excursions to Petra, the UNESCO World Heritage site, where the renowned Treasury and other carved rock walls enchant visitors. Roman ruins like Jerash and Umm Qais exhibit the country's Roman heritage, while the medieval city of Madaba is famed for its mosaic artwork, especially the famous Madaba Map.

Cultural Immersion: Embrace Jordanian culture with packages that include interactions with local communities, traditional music performances, and authentic cuisine experiences. The ancient city of Amman, Jordan's capital, is a vibrant blend of old and new, where travelers can explore busy souks and archaeological sites alongside modern cafes and retail malls.

Desert Adventures: Adventure enthusiasts can select packages that take them to the beautiful Wadi Rum desert. Immersed in spectacular scenery, tourists can experience camel treks, jeep safaris, and stargazing in the immense expanse of sand dunes and rock formations.

Dead Sea Retreats: Tourists looking for leisure can experience the therapeutic benefits of the Dead Sea. The lowest spot on Earth, this salt-laden sea provides buoyant experiences and spa treatments with mineral-rich mud.

Eco-Tourism: Jordan's nature reserves, such as the Dana Biosphere Reserve and Ajloun Forest Reserve, appeal to eco-conscious vacationers. Nature-focused trip programs give opportunities for hiking, bird-watching, and learning about wildlife conservation activities.

Biblical Tours: With connections to biblical stories, Jordan has places including Mount Nebo and Bethany Beyond the Jordan, where Jesus was baptized. These sacred areas lure many religious travelers seeking spiritual experiences.

Adventure Sports: Adventure enthusiasts can indulge in sports like canyoning in Wadi Mujib, diving in the Red Sea near Aqaba, or touring the rock-cut city of Little Petra.

Luxury Travel: For those seeking a premium experience, upmarket tour packages provide top-notch lodgings, private tours, and tailored services, ensuring a memorable stay.

Group Tours: Joining a group trip allows tourists to meet like-minded people from around the world, boosting the social element of the voyage and potentially decreasing costs.

Tailor-Made Tours: Some tour operators provide tailor-made packages, allowing travelers to create their itineraries based on personal preferences and interests.

It's crucial for travelers to assess the duration of the package, inclusions, transportation, and the competence of the trip operator. Moreover, they should be knowledgeable about cultural customs, clothing codes, and entry criteria to provide a smooth and polite encounter.

Conclusion

Jordan's tour package selections cater to a wide range of interests and inclinations, making it a must-visit location for tourists seeking historical, cultural, adventure, and opulent experiences. By picking the correct tour package, travelers may immerse themselves in the delights of Jordan, making experiences that will last a lifetime.

Tourist Safety Tips

As with any trip destination, it's crucial for tourists to prioritize their safety to completely enjoy their experience. Here are tourist safety recommendations in Jordan, letting visitors make the most of their trip while keeping safe and secure.

Cultural Awareness: Jordan is a predominantly conservative Muslim country with stringent social values. Tourists should respect local customs and dress modestly, especially while visiting religious buildings like mosques and churches.

Check Travel Advisories: Before arranging your vacation, it's vital to check for any travel advisories or cautions issued by your government. Stay informed on the current political situation and potential hazards in the region.

Choose Reputable Accommodations: Selecting dependable and well-reviewed hotels is vital for guaranteeing a secure and comfortable stay. Opt for hotels or guesthouses with positive comments from fellow tourists.

Use certified Tour Guides: When exploring historic sites or national parks, consider hiring certified tour guides that have knowledge of the area and can provide helpful insights. This will enhance your experience while minimizing any risks.

Transportation Safety: Only utilize licensed and trustworthy transportation providers, such as registered taxis or recognized automobile rental firms. Ensure that seat belts are available and worn at all times.

Avoid Demonstrations: While Jordan is normally calm, political demonstrations can occur. Avoid joining in or going close to any protests to prevent unintended involvement in potential disruptions.

Be Cautious with Photography: Always ask for permission before taking images of locals, especially women and religious sites. Some areas may have restrictions on photography, so it's important to obey these guidelines.

Be Wary of Scammers: Like any other tourist area, there may be scammers targeting visitors. Be cautious of unsolicited offers and avoid revealing sensitive information to strangers.

Stay Hydrated: Jordan's climate can be harsh, particularly during the summer months. Stay hydrated by drinking plenty of water and avoiding direct sunlight during the warmest portions of the day.

Emergency Contacts: Save crucial phone numbers, such as local emergency services and the nearest embassy or consulate, in case you need assistance.

Keep Valuables Secure: Petty theft can occur in busy locations, so keep your belongings secure and avoid exhibiting expensive items openly.

Stay on Designated Paths: When trekking or visiting natural areas, stick to recognized paths and avoid going off the beaten path to prevent getting lost or meeting dangerous terrain.

Respect Wildlife: Jordan boasts various nature reserves and protected places. While enjoying the natural beauty, refrain from feeding or disturbing the wildlife to protect the ecological balance.

Carry Cash and Identification: Carry a decent amount of cash and identification with you at all times. Use safe money exchange facilities and avoid revealing financial details to strangers.

Secure Your Accommodation: Lock your doors and windows while leaving your accommodation, and utilize the offered safes to store valuables.

Conclusion

By following these tourist safety guidelines in Jordan, travelers can enjoy a satisfying and secure journey across this fascinating country. Embrace the warm welcome of the locals while visiting historic treasures and natural wonders equally, making experiences that will last a lifetime. Remember, responsible travel is not only about protecting the environment and culture but also safeguarding personal safety and well-being.

Festival and Events

From religious observances to cultural festivals, Jordan's calendar is filled with different and vibrant events throughout the year.

One of the major religious festivals in Jordan is Eid al-Fitr, which commemorates the end of Ramadan, the holy month of fasting for Muslims. During this time, families join together to celebrate with feasts, exchange gifts, and engage in charitable deeds. Visitors can witness the festive environment and enjoy the spirit of community and kindness that pervades the country.

Another prominent Islamic celebration is Eid al-Adha, commonly known as the Feast of Sacrifice, remembering Ibrahim's willingness to sacrifice his son. The celebration includes communal prayers, the sacrifice of animals, and the distribution of meat to the less fortunate. This ceremony demonstrates Jordanians' profound attachment to their religious beliefs and the value of family relationships.

The Jerash Festival is a prominent cultural festival conducted yearly in July, celebrating Jordan's rich heritage through music, dance, and theatre performances. The event takes place in the historic Roman city of Jerash, presenting a unique backdrop to the cultural spectacular. Tourists can see traditional folklore, art exhibitions, and handicraft demonstrations, getting insights into Jordan's artistic and historical past.

In Madaba, the Madaba Arts Festival attracts people with its focus on contemporary arts, including local and international artists' works. The festival honors innovation and stimulates cultural interchange, making it a perfect opportunity for travelers to admire modern Jordanian art and connect with the local art scene.

The Al Balad Music Festival, held in Amman, brings together artists and musicians from different backgrounds and genres. It presents a varied spectrum of performances, from traditional Jordanian music to current tunes, allowing an insight into the country's developing musical scene.

For adventure fans, the Amman Marathon offers a unique experience. This annual event gathers runners from around the world and encourages physical fitness and healthy living. Participants can discover the gorgeous streets of Amman while interacting in a pleasant and dynamic atmosphere.

In the city of Aqaba, the Red Sea Winter Art Festival captivates visitors with breathtaking sand sculptures produced by local and international artists. This outdoor show complements Aqaba's magnificent coastal backdrop, allowing travelers to admire art while enjoying the picturesque beaches.

The Jordan Valley International Agricultural Exhibition and Forum provides insights into Jordan's agricultural methods and technologies. This expo showcases agricultural products and innovations, encouraging knowledge exchange among farmers and industry specialists.

Moreover, Jordanian cities like Petra and Wadi Rum often hold events like stargazing evenings and desert festivals, allowing visitors the chance to explore the country's natural treasures in a joyful ambiance.

It's crucial to remember that the festival dates may vary each year, depending on the lunar calendar or unique event organizers. Tourists should check the exact dates before organizing their vacations to guarantee they may engage in these colorful celebrations.

Conclusion

Jordan's festivals and events provide an intriguing insight into the country's rich cultural tapestry and welcoming hospitality. Whether it's experiencing religious observances, touring historical monuments amidst creative displays, or immersing oneself in vivid music and dancing, these festivals offer a fascinating experience for travelers wishing to understand and connect with Jordanian customs and people.

Made in the USA
Las Vegas, NV
14 December 2023

82776165R00069